SCOTNOTE
Number 40

CW00456151

The Gaelic Poetry
of Derick Thomson

Petra Johana Poncarová

Association for Scottish Literary Studies 2020

Published by
Association for Scottish Literary Studies
Scottish Literature
7 University Gardens
University of Glasgow
Glasgow G12 8QH
www.asls.org.uk

ASLS is a registered charity no. SC006535

First published 2020

This work was supported by the European Regional
Development Fund-Project 'Creativity and Adaptability
as Conditions of the Success of Europe in an Interrelated
World' (No. CZ.02.1.01/0.0/0.0/16_019/0000734).

A CIP catalogue for this title
is available from the British Library

ISBN 978-1-906841-43-0

Printed in Great Britain by Bell and Bain Ltd, Glasgow

CONTENTS

SCOTNOTES

Study guides to major Scottish writers and literary texts

Produced by the Education Committee
of the Association for Scottish Literary Studies

Series Editors
Lorna Borrowman Smith
Ronald Renton

THE ASSOCIATION FOR SCOTTISH LITERARY STUDIES aims to promote the study, teaching and writing of Scottish literature, and to further the study of the languages of Scotland.

To these ends, the ASLS publishes works of Scottish literature; literary criticism and in-depth reviews of Scottish books in *Scottish Literary Review*; and scholarly studies of language in *Scottish Language*. It also publishes *New Writing Scotland*, an annual anthology of new poetry, drama and short fiction, in Scots, English and Gaelic. All these publications are available as a single 'package', in return for an annual subscription.

ASLS also produces a range of teaching materials covering Scottish language and literature for use in schools.

Enquiries should be sent to:

ASLS
Scottish Literature
7 University Gardens
University of Glasgow
Glasgow G12 8QH

Tel/fax +44 (0)141 330 5309
e-mail **office@asls.org.uk**
or visit our website at **www.asls.org.uk**

PAGE REFERENCES

CC indicates page references for poems in *Creachadh na Clàrsaich* (Collected Poems 1940–1980). This volume includes the earlier poetry collections *An Dealbh Briste, Eadar Samhradh is Foghar, An Rathad Cian, Saorsa agus an Iolaire* (though sometimes not in their entirety).

SD indicates page references for poems in the collection *Smeur an Dòchais*.

MG indicates page references for poems in the collection *Meall Garbh*.

SF indicates page references for poems in the collection *Sùil air Fàire*.

* English translations marked with an asterisk have been made by the author.

1. INTRODUCTION

As Professor Donald E. Meek expressed it in the eulogy he delivered at Derick Thomson's funeral in 2012, 'Derick Thomson, scholar, teacher, Professor, language planner, poet, businessman, editor, politician, propagandist, chairman of boards and trusts in abundance', was 'uniquely unique'. Derick Thomson, or Ruaraidh MacThòmais, as he preferred to be known in relation to his poetry, was indeed one of the most multi-faceted personalities of Gaelic Scotland in the twentieth century, outstanding not only in terms of his prolific output but also in the scope of his activities, open critical approach and inclusive European outlook. Apart from being an influential university lecturer, scholar, translator and activist, Thomson also contributed to modern Gaelic literature a total of seven poetry collections: the first was published in 1951 and the last appeared in 2007. His career thus spans almost sixty years.

It would be difficult to overstate Thomson's importance in the twentieth-century Scottish Gaelic world. He has been described as the man who did more for the Gaelic language than any other individual in the history of the Gaels and as the father of modern Gaelic publishing. Were he 'only' a poet or an academic, his place in Scottish history would still be secure, but it is his capacity for combining a number of careers and achieving formidable successes in all of them that makes him a unique phenomenon. Two interconnected commitments run through his numerous activities: to revive the Gaelic language and culture and to support Scottish national independence.

In spite of the impressive scope of his work and the seven books of poetry that belong to the peaks of Gaelic literature in the second half of the twentieth century, relatively little

critical attention has been paid to the many aspects of
Thomson's career. Several illuminating studies have been
published but they have far from covered all the elements of
his art and activism, and, for example, his last collection
of poetry has not been subject to any published critical exam-
ination. There has been no critical edition of his poems and
no monograph has been devoted solely to Thomson.

In comparison with Sorley MacLean, whose name has become
synonymous with modern poetry in Scottish Gaelic and who
reached European fame during the last decades of his life,
Thomson seems to be surprisingly neglected. One of the
reasons might be that Thomson died in 2012 and some distance
might still be needed for a genuine evaluation of his achievement. Another might be that in comparison with MacLean,
whose poetry and personality lend themselves more easily to
a romantic identification with the 'authentic voice' of Gaelic
Scotland, Thomson's poetry is quieter and more reticent, and
there is the additional fact that he did not return to live in the
Gaelic-speaking areas and spent most of his life in Glasgow.

This Scotnote seeks to introduce Thomson primarily as a
poet, but it also presents an overview of his life, his political
opinions and his vision of the Gaelic revival, and it mentions
his activities as editor and journalist.

2. BIOGRAPHY OF DERICK THOMSON

Derick Smith Thomson was born on 5 August 1921 in Stornoway in Lewis into a family of Gaelic-speaking intellectuals, and there were teachers and ministers among his ancestors. His parents came from different parts of Lewis and both were Gaelic speakers. He had one older brother, James. Soon after Derick's birth his family moved to Bayble, a township on the Point peninsula, where his father James became headmaster of the local primary school.

James Thomson (Seumas MacThòmais, 1888–1971) came from Tunga near Stornoway. He was a respected poet, the first one ever to receive the Bardic Crown. This was at the National Mòd in 1923 in Inverness. He had a deep interest in Gaelic education and was an active member of An Comunn Gàidhealach (The Gaelic Association). In 1953, a selection of his poetry was published in a volume entitled *Fasgnadh* (*Winnowing*). He also edited a school anthology of Gaelic poetry and co-edited a collection of Lewis songs. Clearly, his father's activities inspired Thomson's own career in many ways.

Thomson's mother, Christina 'Tina' Smith (Tìneag Aonghais Alasdair, 1888–1968), was born in Keose, beside Loch Erisort in Lochs. She was interested in traditional Gaelic poetry and had a large repertoire of Gaelic song. For one year, she studied Celtic at Glasgow University together with her sister, very shortly after women were first allowed to enrol. Before her marriage, she also worked as a schoolteacher. According to Thomson's memories, his mother sang constantly about her work, and he learned many songs from her.

Strictly speaking, Thomson's first language was English and he became bilingual about the age of five, as both languages were spoken in the house. This was deliberate on his parents' part, since most of Lewis was Gaelic-speaking at that time and they thought Gaelic would come easily to the boy in Bayble, while English had to be learned. Later in his life, Thomson tended to speak mostly Gaelic with his mother and English with his father, but his parents had the habit of switching between the two languages continually.

Both his parents were religious, belonging to the Church of Scotland, in which his father was an elder, and so Thomson was not directly exposed to the stricter Presbyterian churches of Lewis, such as the Free Church and other denominations, which shaped the childhood of his Bayble compatriot, the Gaelic poet, playwright and novelist Iain Crichton Smith. Even as a teenager, Thomson was critical of what he considered the extremist branches of evangelical religion in the Highlands and Islands, doubted their presumed 'monopoly on excellence', and later in his life denounced their negative and harmful attitude towards the local culture, such as poetry, music and dance. However, he also admitted that some of the aspects of the religious culture fascinated him and he had great affection for some of the believers he knew, although he did not agree with them.

After leaving the school in Bayble, Thomson studied at the Nicolson Institute in Stornoway and during this period he was drawn to Scottish nationalism. After leaving the Nicolson, Thomson enrolled at the University of Aberdeen for a double degree in English Literature and Celtic. At the university he developed his nationalist stance further by reading pamphlets and works of Scottish literature and meeting prominent nationalist activists, such as Douglas Young, the influential classicist, poet and translator who taught at Aberdeen and was committed to the promotion of both the Scots and Gaelic languages.

Thomson's studies were interrupted by the Second World War. He partly shared the opinion, common among some

Scottish Nationalists at that time, that the war was 'someone else's quarrel' and had no desire to volunteer. He was nonetheless drafted and trained and he served with the Royal Air Force from 1942 to 1945. In an interview for prospective officers, he was asked about the foreign languages he could speak: Thomson promptly listed English and thus his prospects for promotion in the British army ended before they even began. He was stationed in Rodel in Harris and in Point in Lewis and spent his free time reading about Celtic studies, Scottish literature and politics.

In terms of literary influences on Thomson, the Gaelic ones are clear enough. Apart from the folksongs learnt from his mother, Thomson had great interest in and regard for the eighteenth-century poet Alasdair Mac Mhaighstir Alasdair. Mac Mhaighstir Alasdair, with his own deep political commitment and concern for the future of the Gaelic language, was especially close to Thomson's heart and later became a subject of his research, for example in the study *Alasdair Mac Mhaighstir Alasdair: His Political Poetry* (1989). Thomson also valued the other two members of the great eighteenth-century trio, Duncan Ban MacIntyre and William Ross, and considered the eighteenth century the golden age of Gaelic poetry. Among later poets, Thomson appreciated John Smith of Iarsiadar in Lewis, whose political commitment and sense of humour share some features with Thomson's own writing.

Foreign influences on Thomson are more difficult to establish. He was clearly drawn to Welsh literature, with which he also engaged in his research. In the volume of European poetry translated into Gaelic which Thomson edited in 1990 (*Bàrdachd na Roinn-Eòrpa an Gàidhlig/European Poetry in Gaelic*), his own translations include some from old Welsh poetry, Edwin Muir, Hugh MacDiarmid, W. B. Yeats, William Shakespeare, Giacomo Leopardi, R. M. Rilke and Aleksandr

Solzhenitsyn. Thomson also dedicated a poem to Yeats, and mentions him in his reviews for *Gairm* as one of the poets who have fascinated him throughout his life.

After the Second World War, when he graduated with First Class Honours from Aberdeen, Thomson went on to study Anglo-Saxon, Norse and Celtic at the University of Cambridge. His first book, *The Gaelic Sources of Macpherson's 'Ossian'* (1952), was based on the thesis he submitted at Cambridge. It was the first study that actually identified specific Gaelic ballads James Macpherson had drawn on and thus marked a breakthrough in Ossianic studies. Thomson had a deep interest in Ossianic poetry and the related controversies and continued to publish essays on the subject throughout his life.

His first job was Assistant in Celtic at the University of Edinburgh. During this time he also worked as a collector of Gaelic folklore for what was to become the School of Scottish Studies and he travelled to interview tradition bearers. He recorded a number of songs himself and some of them can be heard in the online archive Tobar an Dualchais/Kist o Riches. He then taught at the University of Glasgow and took the opportunity to improve his Welsh during a stay at Bangor. The most substantial academic outcome of Thomson's interest in Welsh language and literature is a highly acclaimed edition of *Branwen Uerch Lyr* (Branwen, Daughter of Llyr) (1961), the second of the Four Branches of the Mabinogi.

In 1951, with Finlay J. Macdonald, Thomson initiated the foundation of *Gairm*, a seminal Gaelic quarterly magazine which lasted for fifty years, and he served as its editor until the last issue. In 1958 the magazine was complemented by Gairm Publications, which went on to produce a wide range of books, including literary works, dictionaries, textbooks and children's literature. In 1952, the same year in which the first issue of *Gairm* appeared, Thomson married Carol Galbraith

(Carol Nic a' Bhreatannaich), originally from Campbeltown, who was a teacher of mathematics and also a Gaelic singer.

It is not well-known that, apart from poetry, Thomson also wrote fiction in Gaelic – and five of his short stories appeared in *Gairm*: 'Foghar 1976' (Autumn 1976, *Gairm* 17); 'Bean a' Mhinisteir' (The Minister's Wife, *Gairm* 22); 'Mar Chuimhneachan' (As a Keepsake, *Gairm* 31); 'Tea Feasgair' (Afternoon Tea, *Gairm* 35); and 'An Staran' (The Stepping Stone, *Gairm* 38). 'Bean a' Mhinisteir' and 'Mar Chuimhneachan' are considered two of the finest Gaelic short stories of the period.

In 1963, Thomson became Professor of Celtic at the University of Glasgow and remained in the position for nearly thirty years, until his retirement in 1991. His most important decision was to place Gaelic literature, rather than the detailed study of the language, at the centre of the curriculum. The department he built in Glasgow contributed to the development of many Gaelic teachers, broadcasters, writers and scholars.

Thomson was crucially involved in the foundation of the Gaelic Books Council in 1968. In addition to that, he published a number of books at the universities where he worked, both in Aberdeen and in Glasgow, and also founded his own separate imprint entitled Clò Chailleann. His *An Introduction to Gaelic Poetry* (1974) and *The Companion to Gaelic Scotland* (edited, 1983) have played a crucial part in making Gaelic literature and culture accessible to the English-speaking world and remain the only publications of their kind to this day, indispensable to all with an interest in Gaelic studies. Thomson also served for many years as President of the Scottish Gaelic Texts Society (Comann Litreachas Gàidhlig na h-Alba) and edited some of its volumes, such as the selected works of Alasdair Mac Mhaighstir Alasdair (1996).

Politics began to play a more important role in Thomson's life in the 1960s and he was active especially in the Pollokshields area of Glasgow. He was even asked to stand for the Scottish National Party as a candidate, but declined, believing that he would make a better contribution to Scotland as an academic. When the Scottish National Party published its Gaelic Policy in 1978, Thomson was one of the main instigators and authors and the topic received substantial coverage in *Gairm*. Thomson supported the cause of Scottish independence throughout his life, even when it was considered peripheral and eccentric, and lived to see the return of the Parliament to Edinburgh in 1999 and the promise of an independence referendum in the near future.

During his lifetime, Derick Thomson received numerous awards, such as the Ossian Prize in 1974 and the Oliver Brown Award in 1984, and he held honorary degrees from various universities. He was elected a Fellow of the Royal Society of Edinburgh in 1977 and of the British Academy in 1992. He died in Glasgow in 2012, at the age of ninety.

3. DERICK THOMSON'S POLITICS

Derick Thomson perceived the United Kingdom as disadvantageous and harmful to the Scottish people and therefore sought to re-establish an independent Scottish state. He adhered to this persuasion throughout his life and saw the gradual transformation of Scottish nationalism from a rather obscure political movement to a major and respectable force in Scottish, British and European politics.

Given the cultural and linguistic diversity of Scotland, Scottish nationalism has not been based on one language and one culture, in contrast to nationalism in Wales or Ireland. There have been attempts to make Gaelic an official language of Scotland, but the fact that there are two candidates for a 'national' language, Gaelic and Scots, has prevented a full-scale adoption of either as a major component of the nationalist campaign.

For a long time, the Highlands and Islands were seen as a separate entity in Scotland and perceived by some as alien and dangerous. They used to belong to the kingdom of Dal Riata, which encompassed parts of today's western Scotland and northeast Ireland, and naturally, there have been strong ties and cultural exchanges with Ireland ever since. Up to 1263, the Hebrides belonged to the Kingdom of Norway. When the Norwegian kings passed the archipelago over to the Scottish crown, the mixed Celtic–Norse population adopted Gaelic culture. It was probably during the period of the Lordship of the Isles when Gaelic culture flourished most, and the powerful Lords of the Isles strove to assert their independence from the Scottish crown as early as the thirteenth century.

The sixteenth century saw the disintegration of Gaelic society in Scotland based on the clan system and on the authority and patronage of the now vanished Lords of the Isles. After the Union of the Crowns in 1603, anti-Celtic policy grew in intensity, taking a distinct shape under King James VI and I in the Statutes of Iona (1609), a set of laws aimed at weakening the Gaelic language and culture and obliterating the overall specific character of the Highlands and Islands and related political threats.

During the seventeenth and eighteenth century, the exiled Stuart dynasty sought and received the support of the Gaels in Scotland and Ireland after they had lost the throne to William of Orange in the 'Glorious Revolution' of 1688. In the popular imagination, the Gaelic-speaking Highlands and Islands became firmly linked with Catholicism and the military threat of the Jacobite risings. Their people, language, and way of life were considered barbarous and alien. When the rising led by the 'Bonnie Prince' Charles Edward Stuart was defeated at Culloden in 1746, the draconian proscription laws introduced by the Westminster government sought to eradicate the distinctiveness of the Gaelic-speaking areas.

During the nineteenth century Gaelic Scotland was further weakened by the Clearances and by massive emigration to the Lowland cities and overseas, especially to Canada and Australia. This dire state became even worse after the First World War, given the high number of Gaels who enlisted in the British army. The losses were in terms of percentage among the highest in the United Kingdom. Ever since the nineteenth century, the number of Gaelic speakers has been steadily dropping.

Thomson's writing may thus be seen as a protest on behalf of the threatened Scottish Gaelic community in Scotland, and the threatened Scottish community in Britain. There are two interrelated loyalties in his works: to the Gàidhealtachd and to Scotland as a whole. In terms of political affiliation Thomson remained faithful to the Scottish National Party throughout his life, supported the efforts to separate Scotland from the

United Kingdom and did not experiment with founding any new political parties which would focus on Gaelic Scotland only. An independent Scottish national state, in charge of its own natural resources and economic policies and firmly linked with Europe, would in Thomson's view provide a safer environment for the further development of its individual languages and cultural traditions, including Gaelic.

In his view, an independent Scotland was important for Gaelic, but Gaelic was also important for Scotland. In the pamphlet *Why Gaelic Matters* Thomson describes Gaelic as 'one of the touchstones of Scottish cultural and political pride', points out that 'the resurgence of interest in Gaelic has close links with various political aspirations for Scotland' and that 'a gradual withering away of a vital part of Scottish history and culture is not to be regarded with equanimity by anyone who has the full interests of Scotland at heart'.[1]

What Thomson emphasised as the most important components of the Gaelic identity were either a command of, or a willingness to learn, the Gaelic language, and historical and cultural awareness. This attitude allowed him to welcome to the Gaelic world people who had learned the language as adults and had come to the culture from the outside. Belonging to Scotland/the Gàidhealtachd, the two communities Thomson pledged his loyalty to, was in his view not governed by blood right or any other inherent quality, but by commitment to the cause.

In spite of the general prominence of traditional culture and literature in the Gaelic world, including academia, Thomson's vision of the Gaelic revival did not rely on folklore. He focused on issues of the present and the future, such as finding vocabulary for modern subjects and situations and publishing new books that would appeal to children and young people and

---

1   Derick Thomson, *Why Gaelic Matters* (Edinburgh: The Saltire Society, 1983), pp. 23, 33.

make them confident and enthusiastic users of Gaelic. His priority was keeping the language alive in the twentieth century and he welcomed the culture which emerged from using the language in new contexts.

Another idea which could seem controversial from the perspective of more traditional revivalists was Thomson's refusal to believe that the best way to support Gaelic was to move to one of the remaining communities where the language is still used, at least to some extent, on a daily basis: '[...] that only by living in a strong Gaelic community can a poet be a spokesman of the Gaelic community. This is palpable nonsense, but it exists.'[2] Thomson himself spent most of his life in Glasgow and never returned to live in his native Lewis. The pronounced intellectualism of his revival, his uncompromising demands for quality in new Gaelic literature and preference for high culture could result in conflicts with those who failed to meet his standards and worked for the Gaelic revival in a more local context and with a less cosmopolitan agenda.

Thomson placed great emphasis on the necessity to communicate with the European tradition and to fight provincialism and narrow-mindedness, to which Gaelic Scotland in his view inevitably – although understandably – tended as a result of its difficult history. In his view, a serious and healthy nationalist persuasion not only did not conflict with pronounced internationalism, but even required it. He therefore supported translations from European languages into Gaelic and sought inspiration for the Gaelic revival in other countries. According to Thomson, confident and diverse nation states that support their various cultures and traditions should inspire and enrich one another, especially in terms of cultural exchanges.

---

2   Derick Thomson, 'Poetry in Scottish Gaelic 1945–1992', *Poetry in the British Isles: Non-Metropolitan Perspectives*, ed. Hans-Werner Ludwig and Lothar Fietz (Cardiff: University of Wales Press, 1995), p. 159.

4. DERICK THOMSON'S POETRY

As Ronald Black has observed, there were two poets who brought twentieth-century Gaelic literature forward 'to the extent that one is at a loss to imagine how it might have looked without them': one is Sorley MacLean, the other Derick Thomson.[3] While MacLean is definitely the more famous and more successful poet when it comes to attracting readers to Gaelic poetry, albeit often via the English translations, Thomson has been more influential as far as the following generations of Gaelic poets are concerned.

Although some of Thomson's early poems were composed in a traditional vein and regular metre, he wrote mostly in carefully crafted free verse and was the first major poet to employ free verse consistently in Gaelic. He also introduced an influential model of what Christopher Whyte describes as a 'caption poem' – a poem which starts with a specific, often sensuous, image, and then an allegorical reading is indicated by a 'caption' at the end.

Thomson's poems come across as muted and unobtrusive, shy of big words and definitive statements, but sometimes fiery indignation flashes through them, especially when the poet discusses politics or examples of injustice towards the Gaels and their language and culture. One of the hallmarks of Thomson's style, which is also evident in his scholarly works and journalism, is his strong sense of humour and delight in mischievous comments. His poetry is also characterised by minute sensitivity to sensuous perceptions and the ability to convey them in a fresh and immediate manner.

Thomson decided to write in Gaelic. He did not have to, for he was equally fluent in both languages, and English was

---

3   Ronald Black, 'Thunder, Renaissance and Flowers', *The History of Scottish Literature. Volume 4: Twentieth Century*, ed. Cairns Craig (Aberdeen: Aberdeen University Press, 1989), p. 201.

technically his first language. His choice to write in Gaelic
was a political act, not a decision of artistic necessity:

> In my case I had decided by that time fairly firmly to make
> Gaelic studies my main career. That reinforced tendencies
> that had been showing up throughout my secondary school,
> nationalistic tendencies if you like, which I think began to
> link by my early teens with the language question. That prob-
> ably had a strong effect in the long run on my choice of Gaelic
> as a creative writing language. [...] I don't think I've ever
> written an original English poem since 1948. I've often
> written translations of my Gaelic poems. Again, there was
> a strongish political motivation behind that, but it wasn't
> the only one. I think there was a strong cultural motivation
> too. I think I felt at that time that whatever I had to say was
> likely to have stronger relevance if it was against a Gaelic
> background.[4]

Thomson translated his own poetry into English and these
translations are usually very successful. One of the reasons
for this translatability is the sensuousness of Thomson's poetry
and his focus on images.

As far as the main themes of Thomson's poetry are concerned,
there are two: places and politics. Especially in his first three
collections, Thomson was extensively preoccupied with his
native island, Lewis. Poetry about places has a long tradition
in Gaelic, and so does writing about one's native place, but
Thomson managed to transform this traditional concern into
something startling and complex, combining traditional
features with modern diction, sociological commentary and
psychological depth. Thomson also became one of the important Gaelic city poets and the focus of his urban poems is

---

4   Derick Thomson, Iain Crichton Smith and Andrew Mitchell, *Taking You Home*
     (Argyll: Argyll Publishing, 2006), p. 95.

Glasgow, the city which has been for centuries absorbing exiles from the Gàidhealtachd and which became the poet's home for most of his life.

The other large preoccupation of Thomson's writing is politics. His large body of work includes poems which comment on specific political issues, such as a referendum or an act of parliament, while others are implicitly political, the meaning is not obvious and has to be inferred, for example, from the context of the whole collection.

Since these two broad topics, places and politics, run through all Thomson's collections, and there is no abrupt change in his interests, it seems more practical and enlightening to follow them throughout his career and to discuss his collections one by one, rather than adopt a thematic approach which would result in two sections of great bulk.

Moreover, since Thomson published quite evenly throughout his life, from his thirties to his late eighties, his books can be read, as Whyte suggests, 'as a single creation, almost a novel, with a plot-like excitement at discovering what became of its initial premises', offering us 'the privilege of insight into how a single mind responded to half a century of Scottish history'.[5]

The following discussion of the poetry is therefore organised according to the eight collections which came out during Thomson's lifetime. The volume of his collected poems, *Creachadh na Clàrsaich/Plundering the Harp*, is treated as a separate collection, for it also contains, apart from almost complete reprints of his first four collections, the section 'Dàin às Ùr' (Latest Poems), some of which had been previously published in magazines but have their only appearance in book-form in this volume. The first four collections are quoted from these collected poems, the last three from the books themselves.

---

5   Christopher Whyte, review of *Smeur an Dòchais*, *Lines Review* 127 (December 1993), p. 49.

An Dealbh Briste (The Broken Picture), 1951

Thomson's first collection of poems, *An Dealbh Briste* (The Broken Picture), appeared in 1951. It allows us to observe Thomson looking for his own distinctive voice as a poet. In the preface, Thomson expresses his belief that 'if Gaelic is to live, it must be written and read, and the idiom of speech and thought that belongs to our time must find some expression in it. Thus, if both my language and my subject matter resemble none too closely the language and subject matter of the old Gaelic bards, I am not, I think, showing in that any disrespect or lack of humility.' He followed this goal, to write in modern Gaelic about current topics, from *An Dealbh Briste* onwards. However, in spite of this statement, there are poems that come very close to traditional Gaelic songs, such as 'Beinn a' Bhuna' (a hill in Lewis, south-west of Stornoway) and 'Smuaintean an Coire Cheathaich' (Thoughts in the Misty Corrie*).

Many of the poems in *An Dealbh Briste* deal with love and disappointment in love. Especially in poems such as 'A' Snìomh Cainnte' (Weaving Words and Weaving Dreams), 'Mur B' e 'n Saoghal is M' Eagal' (Were It Not for the World and My Fear) and ''N e So an Dàn Deireannach Dhut-sa?' (Is This the Last Poem for You?), the collection reveals the strong influence of Sorley MacLean, which Thomson himself acknowledges in the preface to the 1951 edition: we recognise the image of the Cuillin, the link between unfulfilled love and the writing of poetry, and the image of the sweetheart whose beauty has been distracting the speaker from political action. It is well-known that the poets were estranged later in their lives, but in the preface to his first collection Thomson shows great respect and admiration for MacLean, and MacLean was also a regular contributor to *Gairm* in the early years of the magazine's existence.

Another important theme of the collection is concern for Scotland as a nation and for the situation of Gaelic in Scotland.

In 'Smuaintean an Coire Cheathaich' (Thoughts in the Misty Corrie) (CC: 10–11) the speaker revisits a place which has already been firmly embedded in the Gaelic literary tradition, the Misty Corrie which inspired 'Cumha Coire a' Cheathaich' (Lament for the Misty Corrie), one of the famous poems by Duncan Ban MacIntyre, and it is full of echoes of the older poem. The speaker addresses Duncan Ban and contrasts the place as he would have known it with its present state, and extends the adverse change in the Corrie to the Highlands and possibly to Scotland as a whole: 'do dhùthaich bhith fàs, is 'na dìthreabh do mhòinteach, / gun mhàthair ri crònan ach binn-ghlòir nan eun' (your country deserted, and your moorland a wasteland, no mother's humming, only sweet sounds of the birds*). 'Smuaintean an Coire Cheathaich' is, however, also remarkable for the optimism it expresses about the revitalisation of Scotland and, more specifically, of the Gàidhealtachd and the Gaelic language. Although, as the speaker complains to Duncan Ban, there are many who would not understand his poems and who pollute and renounce Gaelic ('cuid a' truailleadh do chainnt 's cuid de d' dhaoine ga h-àicheadh'), he expresses his hope that in the end a change will come over Scotland and the poverty of its lot, and that a new day will break over the rugged corrie.

The love poems and the straightforward patriotic verse represent directions that Thomson did not follow; however, several poems in *An Dealbh Briste* indicate Thomson's mature style as we know it. In 'Pabail' (Bayble) (CC: 42–43), a short poem named after Thomson's native village in Point, his poetry about Lewis starts to emerge as we find in the succeeding poetry collections.

> Air iomall an talamh-àitich, eadar dhà sholas,
> tha a' churracag a' ruith 's a' stad, 's a' ruith 's a' stad,
> is cobhar bàn a broillich, mar rionnag an fheasgair,

ga lorg 's ga chall aig mo shùilean,
is tùis an t-samhraidh
ga lorg 's ga chall aig mo chuinnlean,
is fras-mhullach tonn an t-sonais
ga lorg 's ga chall aig mo chuimhne.

On the edge of the arable land, between two lights, the plover
runs and stops, and runs and stops, the white foam of its
breast like the star of evening, discovered and lost in my
looking, and the fragrance of summer, discovered and lost
by my nostrils, and the topmost grains of the wave of content,
discovered and lost by my memory.

The realistic and intimate focus on sensual perception, a
feature which will be recognised as characteristic of Thomson's
poetry, becomes prominent here. It contains specific, vividly
executed images and a deft connection between the form and
the subject matter, as the timeless rhythms of the sea and of
the regular life in the small community are mirrored in the
regular rhythm of the poem and its repetitions ('a' ruith 's a'
stad' / runs and stops; 'ga lorg 's ga chall' / discovered and
lost). The seamless links between the movements of the plover,
of the sea and of the human life in the village make 'Pabail'
one of the most accomplished poems in the collection.

The highlight of the collection is the poem 'An Tobar' (The
Well) (CC: 48–49), definitely one of Thomson's most successful
early creations. In the poem, the speaker hears about a well
from an old woman:

Tha tobar beag am meadhon a' bhaile
's am feur ga fhalach,
am feur gorm sùghor ga dlùth thughadh,
fhuair mi brath air bho sheann chaillich,

ach thuirt i, 'Tha 'm frith-rathad fo raineach
far am minig a choisich mi le m' chogan,
's tha 'n cogan fhèin air dèabhadh.'
Nuair sheall mi 'na h-aodann preasach
chunnaic mi 'n raineach a' fàs mu thobar a sùilean
's ga fhalach bho shireadh 's bho rùintean,
's ga dhùnadh 's ga dhùnadh.

Right in the village there's a little well
and the grass hides it,
green grass in sap closely thatching it.
I heard of it from an old woman
but she said: 'The path is overgrown with bracken
where I often walked with my cogie,
and the cogie itself is warped.'
When I looked in her lined face
I saw the bracken growing round the well of her eyes,
and hiding it from seeking and from desires,
and closing it, closing it.

The fact that the well is located in the middle of a township, but hidden in lush grass, and that the way to it is overgrown with bracken, suggests that the township is no longer inhabited. It implies that it was deserted as people emigrated, moved to other areas in search of jobs and better services, or the reference may even be to the Clearances. Only the older generation knows about the well and remembers the old way of life. 'An cogan' (the cogie) is a symbol of that way of life, an object of daily use which ceases to be needed in the modern world with running water in houses. As the old woman remarks, no one goes to that well any more, which may refer to both forced and voluntary abandonment of the old way of life, or a combination of both.

'Cha teid duine an diugh don tobar tha sin,'
thuirt a' chailleach, 'mar a chaidh sinne
nuair a bha sinn òg,
ged a tha 'm bùrn ann cho brèagh 's cho geal.'
'S nuair sheall mi troimhn raineach 'na sùilean
chunnaic mi lainnir a' bhùirn ud
a ni slàn gach ciùrradh
gu ruig ciùrradh cridhe.

'Nobody goes to that well now,'
said the old woman, 'as we once went,
when we were young,
though the water is lovely and white.'
And when I looked in her eyes through the bracken
I saw the sparkle of that water
that makes whole every hurt
till the hurt of the heart.

The old woman's speech reminds us of the wealth of the
language which is dying out. She calls the water 'brèagh'
(beautiful) and 'geal' (white). In English, the use of the adjec-
tives for water from the well may sound strange. In Gaelic,
the words are fitting and capture the freshness and purity
of the water. 'Geal', although it denotes white colour, has
also the meaning of 'clear, radiant, bright, glistening'. The
adjective has thoroughly positive connotations in Gaelic,
as it is used in phrases such as 'latha geal' (beautiful day)
and the traditional term of endearment 'gràdh geal mo
chridhe', which translates literally as 'white love of my heart'.
The description is original, fitting and implies an assured
command of the language. The old woman's short phrase stands
for all the things the speaker declares as irretrievably lost at
the end.

'Is feuch an tadhail thu dhomhsa,'
thuirt a' chailleach, 'ga b'ann le meòirean,
's thoir thugam boinne den uisge chruaidh sin
a bheir rudhadh gu m' ghruaidhean.'
Lorg mi an tobar air èiginn
's ged nach b'ise bu mhotha feum air
's ann thuice a thug mi 'n eudail.

Dh'fhaodadh nach eil anns an tobar
ach nì a chunnaic mi 'm bruadar,
oir nuair chaidh mi an diugh ga shireadh
cha d'fhuair mi ach raineach is luachair,
's tha sùilean na caillich dùinte
's tha lì air tighinn air an luathghair.

'And will you go there for me,'
said the old woman, 'even with a thimble,
and bring me a drop of that hard water
that will bring colour to my cheeks.'
I found the well at last,
and though her need was not the greatest
it was to her I brought the treasure.

It may be that the well
is something I saw in a dream,
for today when I went to seek it
I found only bracken and rushes,
and the old woman's eyes are closed
and a film has come over their merriment.

When the speaker is asked to bring a drop of that water to the
old woman, he complies with her request, manages to find
the well and brings her what she has asked for. However,

he suggests that her need was not the greatest. A possible explanation would be that if the water indeed stands for the Gaelic language and culture, the woman, although she has been living outside the natural and cultural environment of her youth, still remembers what it was like and recalls the taste of the water, and so her need is not the greatest – people who are most needful of the refreshing sip are probably those who never experienced it and do not even know they are missing something, possibly people who grow up in Scotland without any knowledge of the Gaelic heritage. Although there is not a single word about language policy and language rights, 'An Tobar' can be read as a powerful comment on the situation of Gaelic.

One of the reasons why the poem is so successful is its imagery. The old woman is visually identified with the well: her eyes, hidden in the bracken of wrinkles, glimmer with life and energy like the water in the well. The notion of closing down and overgrowing runs throughout the poem, connecting the old woman and the place.

Eadar Samhradh is Foghar (Between Summer and Autumn), 1967

Thomson's second collection, *Eadar Samhradh is Foghar* (Between Summer and Autumn), appeared in 1967, sixteen years after *An Dealbh Briste*. After this long pause, during which his poems continued to appear in *Gairm*, Thomson returns as a poet with a voice which is unmistakeably his own and is characterised by conversational tone, humour, attentiveness to detail, distrust of easy optimism, and level-headed awareness of the imperfections of life and humanity.

The first section, 'Eilean an Fhraoich' (Heather Isle), includes mostly poems related to Thomson's relationship to his native island. The opening poem is entitled 'Sgòthan' (Clouds) (CC: 66–67) and it explores, gently and uncompromisingly, the relationship to the native place and the painful changes that may disrupt the fictional image of home when the location is revisited physically and not only mentally.

> Brat ciartha air mo shùil
> air chor 's nach fhaic mi bhuam
> do chaochladh, eilein chiar,
> is m' iargain ort cho buan.

Waxed bandage on my eye, so that I do not see how you have changed, dark island, long missed.

The tone is very direct, as the speaker addresses the place directly with informal singular pronouns that denote intimacy. The poem is much concerned with perception and illusion, with seeing and seeming. The speaker admits that many places in Lewis still seem close to him, but he realises he has strayed from them, so that their nearness proves to be another illusion. These places, once known intimately, have left a deep imprint on the speaker's memory and appear to be easily accessible, yet his decision to leave Lewis, together with the changes that have inevitably occurred in his absence, put them beyond his reach.

The title, 'Sgòthan' (Clouds), indicates instability, constant transformation and also the possibility for the human eye to project into them various shapes of its own fashioning. The clouds that appear repeatedly throughout the six stanzas may stand for the speaker's ambitions and ideas about the world behind the horizon of Lewis, but perhaps the island itself becomes a cloud as well – ungraspable, ever-changing.

As far as form is concerned, the poem is traditional, but in terms of the contradictory feeling and introspective focus, it stands in stark contrast to traditional Gaelic poetry about one's native place, and it provides a telling example of what becomes of the poetry about home in the works of modern

Gaelic poets: other poems dealing with similar issues include
Iain Crichton Smith's 'A' Dol Dhachaigh' (Going Home) and
Donald MacAulay's 'Comharra Stiùiridh' (Landmark).

Another poem concerned with Lewis, 'Clann-nighean an
Sgadain' (The Herring-girls) (CC: 88–89), shows that
Thomson's concern for the place and its people are deeply
intertwined. In this poem, he focuses on the girls and women
who were employed in the fishing industry. In Stornoway, the
herring industry was very important in the latter half of the
nineteenth century, and by the 1870s the town was recognised
as the major herring port of Britain. The herring girls were
women who worked in harbours and waited for ships to arrive
with the catch, their task being to gut the herring and sort
the clean fish into barrels. The work was physically demanding
and financially precarious, as sometimes no catch would be
available, and the workers were paid according to the amount
of fish they processed. Many women from the Gaelic-speaking
areas were employed in the herring trade. Thomson's poem
pays homage to these hard-working women, to their strength
and dignity. The first stanza describes the workers and the
imagery connects them with their occupation:

> An gàire mar chraiteachan salainn
> ga fhroiseadh bho 'm beul,
> an sàl 's am picil air an teanga,
> 's na miaran cruinne, goirid a dheanadh giullachd,
> no a thogadh leanabh gu socair, cuimir,
> [...]
> 's na sùilean cho domhainn ri fèath.

> *Their laughter like a sprinkling of salt*
> *showered from their lips,*
> *brine and pickle on their tongues,*

and the stubby short fingers that could handle fish,
or lift a child gently, neatly,
[...]
and the eyes that were as deep as a calm.

In the second stanza, Thomson comments on the economic exploitation of the Gàidhealtachd and her people. The bustling herring trade did not change the lives of the ordinary workers involved in it: people from the Lowlands and from England benefited from the slavish labour of the locals, who did not enjoy the profits of the natural riches of their home environment, as they did not possess sufficient initial capital to use it.

B' e bun-os-cionn na h-eachdraidh a dh'fhàg iad
'nan tràillean aig ciùrairean cutach,
thall 's a bhos air Galldachd 's an Sasainn.
Bu shaillte an duais a thàrr iad
às na mìltean bharaillean ud,
gaoth na mara geur air an craiceann,
is eallach a' bhochdainn 'nan ciste,
is mara b' e an gàire
shaoileadh tu gu robh an teud briste.

The topsy-turvy of history had made them
slaves to short-arsed curers,
here and there in the Lowlands, in England.
Salt the reward they won
from those thousands of barrels,
the sea-wind sharp on their skins,
and the burden of poverty in their kists,
and were it not for their laughter
you might think the harp-string was broken.

In the third stanza, the speaker notes that these hardships did not break the Gaelic girls and women, who remained strong and managed to keep their families going and to bring up the next generation.

In the second section in this book, 'Gàidhealtachd na h-Albann', the focus moves from the remembrances of things past to the present, and when it dwells on history, it is the public history rather than the private one, and always with relevance to the present state of affairs. The opening poem, 'A' Ghàidhealtachd' (The Highlands) (CC: 92–93), presents a gloomy image of a deserted house filled with rotting furniture which becomes a symbol of the dismal state of the Highlands. Other poems included in the section, such as 'Am Prionnsa Teàrlach' (Prince Charlie) (CC: 96–97), 'Cruaidh?' (Steel?) (CC: 98–99) and 'Anns a' Bhalbh Mhadainn' (lit. 'In the dumb morning', translated by the poet himself as 'Sheep') (CC: 98–99), comment from various angles on the current crisis in the region and its historical roots.

This section also contains one of the best modern poems dealing with the topic of the Clearances: 'Srath Nabhair' (Strathnaver) (CC: 94–95). The title announces a distinct location, Strathnaver, and to those acquainted with Highland history the place name immediately evokes the infamous clearances that occurred on the Sutherland estate in the first half of the nineteenth century, and the series of discussions and accusations they have been provoking ever since.

The poem begins with the speaker looking back on what was probably the clearing of his family and the burning of their house, as was sometimes the practice during the evictions in order to prevent the displaced people from returning to their former dwellings, as wood was scarce in the Highlands and Islands and difficult to obtain.

Anns an adhar dhubh-ghorm ud,
àirde na sìorraidheachd os ar cionn,
bha rionnag a' priobadh ruinn
's i freagairt mireadh an teine
ann an cabair taigh m' athar
a' bhliadhna thugh sinn an taigh le bleideagan sneachda.

In that blue-black sky,
as high above us as eternity,
a star was winking at us,
answering the leaping flames of fire
in the rafters of my father's house,
that year we thatched the house with snowflakes.

At the very start, the connection between a burning house in the Highlands and a distant star in the vast night sky gives the scene a universal scope. The idea of thatching the destroyed home with snowflakes is a moving comment on the helplessness of those affected by the evictions. In the second stanza, the poem proceeds to bring forth the topsy-turvy priorities of the Clearances and the hypocrisy of their executors by means of referring ironically to the Gospel of Matthew (8:20): 'Foxes have holes, and birds of the air have nests; but the Son of Man hath not where to lay his head.'

Agus siud a' bhliadhna cuideachd
a shlaod iad a' chailleach don t-sitig,
a shealltainn cho eòlach 's a bha iad air an Fhìrinn,
oir bha nid aig eunlaith an adhair
(agus cròthan aig na caoraich)
ged nach robh àit aice-se anns an cuireadh i a ceann
    fòidhpe.

And that too was the year
they hauled the old woman out on to the dung-heap,
to demonstrate how knowledgeable they were in Scripture,
for the birds of the air had nests
(and the sheep had folds)
though she had no place in which to lay down her head.

Thomson's bracketed note that the sheep had folds is a subtle hint, very typical of the poet, at the fact that the main reason for the Clearances was the introduction of big and profitable sheep farms and that the needs of the sheep and their owners were therefore prioritised over the needs of the people.

In the last stanza, the speaker addresses two straths affected by the clearances, Strathnaver and Strath of Kildonan, and points out that the unique, wild landscape of the Highlands and Islands, void of human presence and so appealing to visitors today, is a result of painful, controversial historical events:

A Shrath Nabhair 's a Shrath Chill Donnain,
is beag an t-iongnadh ged a chinneadh am fraoch àlainn oirbh,
a' falach nan lotan a dh'fhàg Pàdraig Sellar 's a sheòrsa,
mar a chunnaic mi uair is uair boireannach cràbhaidh
a dh'fhiosraich dòrainn an t-saoghail-sa
is sìth Dhè 'na sùilean.

O Strathnaver and Strath of Kildonan,
it is little wonder that the heather should bloom on your slopes,
hiding the wounds that Patrick Sellar, and such as he, made,
just as time and time again I have seen a pious woman
who has suffered the sorrow of this world
with the peace of God shining from her eyes.

'Am fraoch àlainn' (the beautiful heather) is hiding the wounds made by the perpetrators of the Clearances, such as the Sutherland estate factor Patrick Sellar. Evictions of the people who used to live in Strathnaver and Kildonan are presented as wounds on the place itself and this image of the wounded landscape is another manifestation of the inseparable link between the place and its people in Thomson's poetry. Strathnaver and Kildonan are locations loaded with historical meaning. Interestingly, it is an absence that commemorates the traumatic events in Thomson's poem: the slopes on which heather covers the 'wounds', i.e. places where human dwellings used to stand, function as memorials to the evicted communities. The awareness of these voids, of an emptiness that should not be there, keeps the memory of the Clearances alive. Thomson presents no grand redemptive vision: only a bitter and resolute statement about a historical act of injustice which should serve as fuel for decisive political action in the present and in the future.

The collection also contains several poems which can be read as more or less covert comments on the situation of the Gaelic language. 'Uiseag' (Lark) (CC: 104–05) is a typical representative of the 'caption poem' mentioned earlier. The first part describes a seemingly straightforward image, that of a wounded bird:

A' plosgartaich air an fheur an sin,
air do chliathaich,
na h-asnaichean beaga ag èirigh 's a' tuiteam,
is strìochag dhubh-dhearg air an iteig,
's do shùilean a' call an sgèanachd,
tha do latha dheth seachad,
is dè math bhith gad iargain?

Throbbing there on the grass,
lying on your side,
the little ribs rising and falling,
and a dark-red streak on the wing,
and with the frightened look leaving your eyes,
it's all over with you,
and what's the good of mourning?

However, instead of continuing the story, the second stanza takes one step back and starts to suggest a symbolic meaning to the previously introduced image.

Ach ged a theireadh mo reusan sin rium,
's ged tha 'n fhuil tha mu mo chridhe a' reodhadh
brag air bhrag, is bliadhn' air bhliadhna,
cluinnidh mi i ag èigheachd ris a' chuimhne
'O! na faiceadh tu i air iteig
cha sguireadh tu ga h-ionndrain gu sìorraidh.'

But though my reason might say that to me,
and though the blood around my heart is freezing –
year upon year I hear its sharp reports –
yet still it shouts to the memory
'O! could you but have seen her on the wing
you would go on longing for her for ever.'

According to Christopher Whyte, the poem can be read as an allegory of the Gaelic language:

The notion that the speaker is suffering the same fate as the skylark is startling, and the information demands to be integrated as part of our overall understanding of the poem [...] It is the overall context of the other poems in the book, as well as the larger context within which we read the book,

that prompts one to attach a meaning such as "Gaelic culture",
or "the Gaelic language", to the bird and its imminent demise.[6]

Indeed, when one reads 'Uiseag' in the context of the whole
collection, one quite naturally comes to the conclusion that
the poem should be understood as a more covert comment on
the same themes as the other poems.

A similar strategy is employed in the poem 'Anns a' Bhalbh
Mhadainn' (Sheep) (CC: 98–99), only the allegorical meaning
is suggested in a more straightforward manner. In this case,
the opening image appears to be a memory from the family
croft when sheep got lost on the moor in a sudden snowstorm.
It is revealed, however, that the storm did not affect only one
region but the whole country, with deadly and smothering
snow, which is also deceptive. The speaker then states that he
would rejoice if he saw a yellow spot on the white plain and
knew there the Gaels were still breathing. The snow can,
and must therefore be, interpreted in terms of language and
culture. Introducing extensive sheep farms in the Highlands
and Islands was, of course, the main motive behind the
Clearances and thus one of the chief impulses which led to
the desolation of Gaelic language and culture in the nineteenth
century, and so the connection is deeply ironical.

The weakening of Gaelic is also the subject of the poem
'Cainnt nan Oghaichean' (Grandchildren's Talk) (CC: 92–93),
one of Thomson's short masterpieces:

Nuair a thig am feasgar cuiridh sibh làmh anns a' phutan,
is their sibh gun d' fhuair sibh solas,
buidheachas do Dhia is do Chalum MacMhaoilein.
Is dòcha gum bi sgeul eile aig na h-oghaichean
nuair a bhios iad 'nan cailleachan 's 'nam bodaich:

---

6   Christopher Whyte, 'Derick Thomson: The Recent Poetry', *Aiste* 1 (2007), p. 23.

iad ag èisdeachd an oghaichean fhèin, na coigrich bheaga,
a chaill cainnt am màthar, is beus an daoine,
's ag ràdh, gach aon 'na aonar,
'Chuir sinne an solas às.'

When evening comes you will press the switch,
and say that the light has come,
thanks to God and to Malcolm Macmillan.
Perhaps the grandchildren will think otherwise
when they are old men and women:
listening to their own grandchildren, the little strangers,
who have lost their mother tongue, and their people's virtues,
and saying, each one alone,
'We put out the light.'

Thomson himself pointed out that 'the coming of electric
light is used as an ironic image of "progress" which has as its
accompaniment (factual but not causal) language decline'.[7]
The poem is a comment on the paradoxical consequences
of technological progress which brings about distinct
improvements in the material aspects of life, but the adoption
of the modern conveniences also leads to the adoption of
a new language and culture and to the decline of the local
heritage.

The collection closes with one of Thomson's most famous
and critically acclaimed poems, 'Cisteachan-laighe' (Coffins)
(CC: 122–23). It is remarkable for its successful combination
of subtle form, sensual immediacy and vivid imagery with
political message. The poem was inspired by Thomson's
maternal grandfather who lived in Keose and was, among
many other activities, a joiner and a coffin maker. As Thomson

---

7   Derick Thomson, 'Tradition and Innovation in Gaelic Verse since 1950',
    Transactions of the Gaelic Society of Inverness LIII (1982–1984), p. 101.

mentioned in an interview, the immediate impulse for writing
the poem was the publication of the 1961 Census numbers of
Gaelic speakers, which revealed a considerable drop from the
previous census ten years before.

One of the important factors behind this attrition was
the 1872 Education (Scotland) Act which effectively banned
Gaelic from schools. Such pressure on the part of the authorities was still felt strongly in the first half of the twentieth
century and in the opinion of some continued to be applied,
although more subtly and with less open hostility, in the second
half. It was only after the 1918 Education Act (Scotland)
was passed that Gaelic gained recognition in law but, as its
treatment of Gaelic was vague and brief, this piece of legis-
lation had little real impact.

The poem opens with a specific image of a man with a beard
working with a plane. This is a memory of the speaker's grandfather – every time he passes a joiner's shop in the street,
the smell of sawdust reminds him of his grandfather's
workshop.

> Duin' àrd, tana
> 's fiasag bheag air,
> 's locair 'na làimh:
> gach uair thèid mi seachad
> air bùth-shaoirsneachd sa' bhaile,
> 's a thig gu mo chuinnlean fàileadh na min-sàibh,
> thig gu mo chuimhne cuimhne an àit ud,
> le na cisteachan-laighe,
> na h-ùird 's na tairgean,
> na sàibh 's na sgeilbean,
> is mo sheanair crom,
> is sliseag bho shliseag ga locradh
> bhon bhòrd thana lom.

Mus robh fhios agam dè bh' ann bàs;
beachd, bloigh fios, boillsgeadh
den dorchadas, fathann den t-sàmhchair.
'S nuair a sheas mi aig uaigh,
là fuar Earraich, cha dainig smuain
thugam air na cisteachan-laighe
a rinn esan do chàch:
'sann a bha mi 'g iarraidh dhachaigh,
far am biodh còmhradh, is tea, is blàths.

A tall thin man
with a short beard,
and a plane in his hand:
whenever I pass
a joiner's shop in the city,
and the scent of sawdust comes to my nostrils,
memories return of that place,
with the coffins,
the hammers and nails,
saws and chisels,
and my grandfather, bent,
planing shavings
from a thin, bare plank.

Before I knew what death was;
or had any notion, a glimmering
of the darkness, a whisper of the stillness.
And when I stood at his grave,
on a cold Spring day, not a thought
came to me of the coffins
he made for others:
I merely wanted home
where there would be talk, and tea, and warmth.

The speaker mentions only one kind of wooden item his grandfather used to make – coffins – and then lists some of the tools he used to see in his workshop, such as chisels, hammers and saws. This indicates that the main preoccupation of the poem is death, on many levels – death of the speaker's grandfather, death of his childhood innocence, premonition of his own death, language and culture death, and death as a general phenomenon determining human existence.

The end of the first stanza returns to the opening image of the speaker's grandfather – the old man planing shavings from a thin, bare plank. The notion of baring and shaving, removing layers, of course does not apply only to wooden material: it concerns the life of the grandfather, from which year after year is shaved, the speaker's own childhood innocence, from which experience removes one shaving after another, his own life, and also the diminishing numbers of Gaelic speakers in the final stanza:

> Is anns an sgoil eile cuideachd,
> san robh saoir na h-inntinn a' locradh,
> cha tug mi 'n aire do na cisteachan-laighe,
> ged a bha iad 'nan suidhe mun cuairt orm;
> cha do dh'aithnich mi 'm brèid Beurla,
> an lìomh Gallda bha dol air an fhiodh,
> cha do leugh mi na facail air a' phràis,
> cha do thuig mi gu robh mo chinneadh a' dol bàs.
> Gus an dainig gaoth fhuar an Earraich-sa
> a locradh a' chridhe;
> gus na dh'fhairich mi na tairgean a' dol tromham,
> 's cha shlànaich tea no còmhradh an cràdh.

> *And in the other school also,*
> *where the joiners of the mind were planing,*

I never noticed the coffins,
though they were sitting all round me;
I did not recognise the English braid,
the Lowland varnish being applied to the wood,
I did not read the words on the brass,
I did not understand that my race was dying.
Until the cold wind of this Spring came
to plane the heart;
until I felt the nails piercing me,
and neither tea nor talk will heal the pain.

The 'joiners of the mind' in the 'other school' are the education authorities striving to plane Gaelic off the children's brains and hearts, and the children sitting in the school desks thus become coffins in which their dying culture and language are going to be buried. The coffins are adorned with English braid, the varnish applied to the wood is 'Gallda' (meaning both Lowland and foreign, alien, non-native). The speaker as a boy did not read the words on the brass plate and he did not understand what was happening to his people. In this line, Thomson translates the word 'cinneadh' as 'race' and it is indeed used in that sense in modern Gaelic (for example, racism is 'gràin-cinnidh', lit. 'hatred of race'), but its meaning in Gaelic, according to Edward Dwelly's dictionary, includes also 'clan, tribe, surname, relations, kin, kindred'. Arguably, what the speaker mourns here is not the death of some presumed pure race of the Gaels, but the death of language and culture which were the most important components of Gaelic identity in Thomson's view.

An Rathad Cian (The Far Road), 1970

Thomson's third poetry collection, *An Rathad Cian* (The Far Road), appeared in 1970 and is devoted entirely to Lewis

— the dedication even introduces the book 'mar thiodhlag do eilean m' àraich, Leòdhas' (as an offering to the island of my upbringing, Lewis). The other dedicatee is the poet's deceased mother and Thomson mentioned that the death of his mother was an important impulse for the creation of *An Rathad Cian*. The maternal and funeral imagery is very prominent in the collection. The book contains fifty-six poems exploring different aspects of the island, its landscape, history and people. The local rootedness of the collection is also manifested in the language, for Gaelic has a very fine shading of local accents and dialects, delineating not only islands but even villages, and the colouring in terms of recognisably Lewis Gaelic is fairly strong in the volume. Thomson himself commented on the collection:

> I have had a long love affair with Lewis, and a long interest in trying to describe and comment on the experience of living there. It may well have been that round about this time, in the middle '60s, I was coming to the view that central though it was to my experience, it wasn't something I was ever likely to go back to in any physical sense.[8]

The opening poem, 'An Uilebheist' (The Monster) (CC: 126–27), and the final one, 'An Ceann Thall' (The Far Side) (CC: 174–75), frame the collection as a dialogue between the speaker and the island, and Lewis is addressed in various guises: as a stone, a boat, a loom, and a sea monster. The imagery is also local and the collection is thus, literally, all about the island.

The opening poem sets up three essential characteristics of the whole sequence: its religious dimension, the ambiguous

---

8   Christopher Whyte and Derick Thomson, 'Interviews with Ruaraidh MacThòmais', *Glasgow: Baile Mòr nan Gàidheal/City of the Gaels*, edited by Sheila M. Kidd (Glasgow: Roinn na Ceiltis, Oilthigh Ghlaschu, 2007), p. 242.

relationship to the island and the therapeutic function of the
collection:

> Ag èirigh à muir uaine
> cobhar-shrianagach an Fhoghair,
> air d' uilinn,
> O uilebheist mo dhomhain,
> tha mi tighinn thugad le m' adhradh,
> le mo shùilean prabach, leis a' chainnt
> a dh'ionnsaich mi aig d' altair,
> leis na briathran
> a choisrig mi 'na do sheirbheis,
> leis a' cheòl
> a chuaileanaich ma mo chluasan [...]

> *As you rise from the green sea,*
> *foam-streaked with Autumn,*
> *on your elbow,*
> *O monster of my world,*
> *I come to you in worship,*
> *with red-rimmed eyes, a language*
> *learnt at your altar,*
> *the words*
> *I consecrated to your service,*
> *the music*
> *that stole upon my hearing* [...]

As it sometimes is, the word 'uilebheist' is treated as feminine
in terms of grammatical gender, so the island becomes a
feminine entity – later in the collection, it is indeed addressed
as a mother and as female lover. Lewis is thus first invoked as
a monster arising from the sea, which is a fitting image for
an island, especially given the colour of Lewis, but it also
reveals something essential about the speaker's relationship

to the place. The island is the speaker's obsession, something that terrifies him but at the same time captivates and binds him. From the opening poem, the island emerges as an all-pervasive influence: the language of the poem is that which the speaker learned at the monster's altar, the words are consecrated to its service. Yet these words are not going to be ones of easy praise, as the rest of the poem makes clear:

leis a' mheirg air mo bhilean,
leis a' ruithleum, leis a' bhàs
a dh'fhuiling mi air do sgàth,
leis a' bhrèig, leis an taise,
le do mhaise ga mo mhealladh,
leis a' chruas, leis a' chràdh,
leis a' chuimhne, leis a' chridhe,
leis a' chridhe sin a chailleadh,
leis a' chaille-chridhe-bianain,
leis a' mharcan-seachran-sìne,
leis an earball-saillte-sàile,
leis an fhuidheall dhe mo ghràdh dhut.

the rust on my lips,
the élan, the death
I suffered for your sake,
the lies, the sentiment,
your beauty blinding me,
the hardness, the pain,
the memory, the heart,
that heart I forfeit,
phosphorescent heart,
spendthrift spindrift,
salt-tail-tangle,
remnant of my regard for you.

The ambiguous relationship to the place is proclaimed at the very beginning. In the list of items the speaker acquired from the island/monster and which he brings to its shrine, one finds gifts and blessings, but also restrictions, injuries and deceit. 'An fhuidheall dhe mo ghràdh dhut' (remnant of my regard for you) indicates the uneasiness, the gradual sobering up and tearing of the ties of the obsessive concern the relationship with Lewis has for him. It is, in accordance with the author's comments, portrayed as a love affair. But the remnant of the regard is still powerful enough to fuel the fifty-six poems of the collection, which are passionate, tender and sometimes bitterly critical, but never indifferent.

In several poems, such as 'Chaill Mi Mo Chridhe Riut' (I Lost My Heart to You) (CC: 132–33) and 'Leannan M' Òige' (Sweetheart of My Youth) (CC: 128–29), Lewis emerges in the guise of a lover. The moorland-covered island is personified as a girl with 'do chuailean donn' (your brown hair) and 'do shùilean dorcha' (your dark eyes) and its landscape with mounds and hollows becomes the body of a woman.

In 'Dh'fhairich Mi Thu le Mo Chasan' (I Got the Feel of You with My Feet) (CC: 130–31), the island becomes a woman again, but this time it is a mother allowing a child to find peace and security. The poem moves between the island past and the city present. The difference in lifestyle, environment and age is summed up in the memory of going barefoot: 'Dh'fhairich mi thu le mo chasan / ann an toiseach an t-samhraidh; / m'inntinn an seo anns a' bhaile / a' strì ri tuigse, 's na brogan a' tighinn eadarainn' (I got the feel of you with my feet, / in early summer; / my mind here in the city / strives to know, but the shoes come between us). In this poem, the possible reconciliation with the place is hinted at:

is bhon a tha an saoghal a bh'againn
a' leantainn ruinn chon a' cheum as fhaide

chan fhiach dhomh am poll sin a ghlanadh
tha eadar òrdagan a' bhalaich.
Agus a-nis aig meadhon latha,
tha mi dol a-steach gha mo gharadh,
le mo chasan-rùisgte air fàd ri taobh na cagailt.

and since the world we knew
follows us as far as we go
I need not wash away that mud
from between the boy's toes.
And now, in middle age,
I am going in to warm myself,
with my bare feet on a peat beside the hearth.

There is no need to 'wash away that mud': to forget his island childhood is impossible and the memories can moreover provide warmth even when the speaker has grown up and left the place.

An Rathad Cian does not present a story of gradual abandonment, of finding a solution. It is tied together by repetitions and motifs that are picked up across the fifty-six poems. This tidal movement of coming closer and withdrawing, praise and critique, love and hate, obsession and disillusionment, allows the speaker, in the end, to leave the monster's temple.

'"Burn is Mòine 's Coirc"' ("Water and Peats and Oats") (CC: 130–31) introduces the city as a counterpoint to the island, as a place where the remembering of Lewis takes place. The overheard words of a stranger, 'water and peats and oats', represent some of the most essential daily realities of island life and instantly trigger old memories. This automatic reaction of the speaker, that a few words suffice to transport him back to the place he left long ago, appears to him as 'boile' (madness): 'An cridhe gòrach / a' falpanaich mu na seann stallachan ud / mar nach robh slighe-cuain ann / ach i' (The foolish heart, / lapping along these ancient rocks / as though there were no

sea-journey in the world / but that one). His own attachment
to the place seems extreme to him, yet he cannot help the
spontaneous reaction of his emotions: for his heart, there is
still no sea journey in the world but the one leading to Lewis.

At the end of the short poem, Thomson uses a very specific,
physical and local image and plain, everyday words that would
have been common in the village to communicate the painful
attachment. The heart is tied to a tethering post, 'car ma char
aig an fheist / 's i fàs goirid' (round upon round of the rope /
till it grows short), and the mind is free, yet its freedom has
been achieved at a great cost: 'is daor a cheannaich mi a saorsa'
(I bought its freedom dearly). The dearly bought freedom refers
to the decision to leave the island, to get education and a job
and another life outside it and break the bond.

The theme of exile is not treated by Thomson only as a private
predicament through adopted personalities, but as a situation
common to other Lewis people and as a process which has been
shaping the history of the island. The poem 'Na Lochlannaich
a' Tighinn air Tìr an Nis' (The Norsemen Coming Ashore
at Ness) (CC: 160–61) presents an unusual view of the
Scandinavian incomers to the Western Isles and adds another
important piece to the overall tapestry of Lewis which *An
Rathad Cian* unfolds: the Scandinavian influence on the Gaelic
world which is so strong especially in Lewis, in place names
and also in the local dialect of Gaelic. In this poem, just as in
many later ones, Thomson provides parallels with the Gaelic
situation. This time, it is not the Gaels who come ashore to
settle in a new strange land, an image common in the songs of
the emigrants, but the Norsemen. Apart from disrupting the
stereotypical image of the Scandinavian incomers as plun-
derers by presenting them as people who were afraid and later
settled down as farmers, Thomson also, contrary to many a
song and poem of the Gaelic tradition, suggests that people
can get used to their new environment and be content with it

– that the homesickness will go away after some time ('agus dh'fhalbh an cianalas'). He uses the image of the Norsemen to show that the homesickness does not last forever, that people do eventually settle down, get used to their new environment, and start a life with what is at hand.

Another important part of Thomson's portrayal of the island is the religious climate. One of Thomson's main objections was that the evangelical churches often strove to suppress the traditional folk culture and in consequence weakened the language:

> The evangelical religion arrived somewhat late in Lewis, but we have accounts from the third and fourth decades of the nineteenth century of evangelical ministers stamping as hard as they could on local culture. Ordering people to break their fiddles and break their pipes and stop singing vain songs.[9]

Calvinism also helped to loosen the strong cultural links with Catholic Ireland. This point of view is expressed most strongly in 'Am Bodach-Ròcais' (Scarecrow) (CC: 140–41).

The poem describes a situation when a black-haired man, an evangelical minister or preacher, arrives at a ceilidh house where people are sitting round the fire and engaging in traditional community amusements ('ceilidh' means a visit and also a community gathering with singing and storytelling). The image of the minister draws on the tradition of portraying the representatives of evangelical churches in the Highlands as sinister, ominous dark figures who kill all joy:

An oidhch' ud
thàinig am bodach-ròcais dhan taigh-chèilidh:
fear caol àrd dubh

---

9 Derick Thomson, Iain Crichton Smith and Andrew Mitchell, *Taking You Home*, p. 97.

is aodach dubh air.

Shuidh e air an t-sèis

is thuit na cairtean às ar làmhan.

Bha fear a siud

ag innse sgeulachd air Conall Gulban

is reodh na faclan air a bhilean.

Bha boireannach 'na suidh' air stòl

ag òran, 's thug e 'n toradh às a' cheòl.

That night

the scarecrow came into the ceilidh-house:

a tall, thin, black-haired man

wearing black clothes.

He sat on the bench

and the cards fell from our hands.

One man

was telling a folktale about Conall Gulban

and the words froze on his lips.

A woman was sitting on a stool,

singing songs, and he took the goodness out of the music.

The poem has an almost filmic quality to it or it could very easily serve as a subject for a painting: the moment the black-haired figure enters the cosy house, everything freezes, cards fall down, and chatter dies out. In spite of the derogatory title of 'Scarecrow', the man's presence is powerful and transformative – the music loses its goodness, all the activities cease. The black-haired man is also giving, not only taking away, yet the gifts are destructive:

Ach cha do dh'fhàg e falamh sinn:

thug e òran nuadh dhuinn,

is sgeulachdan na h-àird an Ear,

is sprùilleach de dh'fheallsanachd Geneva,

is sguab e 'n teine à meadhon an làir
's chuir e 'n tùrlach loisgeach nar broillichean.

But he did not leave us empty-handed:
he gave us a new song,
and tales from the Middle East,
and fragments of the philosophy of Geneva,
and he swept the fire from the centre of the floor
and set a searing bonfire in our breasts.

The strength of the poem lies in the striking visual image it conveys and also in the ironic correlations between the traditional folk culture and the imported culture of evangelical Christianity: the richness of Gaelic songs is replaced by a new song, which is an echo of Psalm 40 ('He gave me a new song to sing'), the tales of ancient kings and heroes by Biblical stories, and the community and its solidarity by fragments of Calvinist philosophy. The word 'sprùilleach', which means crumbs, fragments or refuse, indicates that what the scarecrow brings is not even a proper philosophical system which would replace the traditional mind-set but debris which could have been twisted and misinterpreted on the way.

The final image of the change from the homely fire in the middle of the ceilidh house, which drew the people together and provided light and warmth for the assembled community, to the individual searing bonfires of fear of damnation in the breast of each individual, a divisive flame of fanaticism, is especially powerful. The bonfire could also bring to mind the widespread image of a fire used for burning musical instruments by converts seized by evangelical zeal.

A more humorous and tongue-in-cheek take on the island's religion is presented in the poem 'A' Cluich air Football le Fàidh' (Playing Football with a Prophet) (CC: 134–35). The

poem begins with the speaker's statement that when one has
ever played football with a prophet, it is an unforgettable
experience.

'S ann air fàidhean an Aonaidh a b' eòlaich mi,
ach thuig mi, gu math tràth,
gu robh fàidhean anns an Eaglais Shaoir cuideachd,
fàidhean ann am Barraigh
agus eadhon anns an Eilean Sgitheanach,
agus beag air bheag thuig mi
nach robh tròcair an Tighearna air a cuingealachadh
ri creud no ceàrnaidh
no eadhon cànan.
'S e 'm peacadh as motha
a bhith càrnadh a' ghràis gu lèir 'na do chliabh fhèin.

I was better acquainted with Church of Scotland prophets,
but understood, quite young,
that there were prophets in the Free Church too,
prophets in Barra,
and even in Skye,
and bit by bit I came to know
that the Lord's mercy is not confined
by creed or region,
or even language.
The greatest sin
is to pile all of the Grace in your own creel.

The surprising discovery that there are prophets in churches
other than the established one (even among the Catholic clergy!)
and in other places than Lewis is a satirical reference to the
sectarian strains in Highland religion and also to the rivalry
between the individual islands. The final conviction about the
unlimited range and reach of divine grace, expressed through

the particular and very day-to-day image of the creel, as if mercy came into the world in the form of peat turfs, is at the same time amusing and poetically convincing.

In spite of these critical comments, Thomson is not an anti-religious poet and in some later poems, such as in 'Àirc a' Choimhcheangail' (The Ark of the Covenant) (CC: 268–69), he expresses a great deal of sympathy for the Lewis manifestations of Christianity – however, this sympathy seems to be directed mainly at the common believers, their strength and human dignity, never at the dogmas.

The resolution, perhaps even mutual absolution between the place and the speaker, is woven into the sequence, and so it does not appear as a surprise at the end. In 'An Ceann Thall' (CC: 174–75) he emerges from the monster's temple, ready to get on with his life. Indeed, in the following collections, Lewis does not loom as large, although it continues to be present. It becomes one theme among others, not a monster of the poet's world. As Thomson himself pointed out, *An Rathad Cian* is not just a personal farewell to an island – it is a farewell to a whole way of life, to the mostly lost world of the traditional Gaelic communities where he grew up.

Saorsa agus an Iolaire (Freedom and the Eagle), 1977

According to the cover note on Thomson's next collection, *Saorsa agus an Iolaire* (Freedom and the Eagle), most of the poems contained within are 'situated in the present and they also look forward to the future'. Published seven years after *An Rathad Cian*, it marks Thomson's move from the past to the present, from the personal to the public, and from the Gàidhealtachd to Scotland as a whole. It is the most overtly political collection Thomson ever published, which has also been noted by his contemporary reviewers and later critics. This is not surprising given the developments in the 1970s: North Sea Oil was discovered, the Scottish National Party was on the rise, and Thomson was involved in campaigning during the General Elections of 1974 and in local elections.

Saorsa agus an Iolaire is also Thomson's most difficult collection to approach. While the previous collections usually provided the readers with rather clear indications as to how to interpret some of the allegorical poems, in this volume the tone is much more obscure and less reader-friendly. It also introduces a new formal preference of Thomson's for the poem-sequence. *An Rathad Cian* was a book-length sequence, but in this collection several longer poems appear, such as 'An Turas' (The Journey), 'An Tobar' (The Well), 'An Iolaire' (The Eagle) and 'An Crann' (The Plough), allowing Thomson to pursue one theme at greater length and approach it from different perspectives.

Many of the poems abound in puns and wordplay and contain some references which imply a political meaning which remains nonetheless hard to establish. They include 'Alb'-Chalg' (Scots-Stab) (CC: 190–91), where the explanation is contained only in the last line 'Alb'-chalg a bh'ann – / cha dean Galla-phlàsd feum dha' (Scots-stab it was – foreign plaster doesn't help it.). The poem 'Fuil' (Blood) (CC: 188–89) may not seem political at first glance, but in connection with another poem in the collection, 'Rabhadh' (Warning) (CC: 190–91), it is possible to read it politically, for both poems mention labour and birth which is apparently not human but rather communal and national. In 'Sgeulachd Albannach' (A Scottish Story) (CC: 194–95) the political meaning must be inferred from a reference to the legend according to which Robert Bruce, while hiding after the defeat at Methven and despondent, observed a spider continually remaking its web in a cave, and, drawing inspiration from the patient arachnid, decided to keep up his own tiring struggle and free Scotland from English rule.

The sequence 'An Iolaire' (The Eagle) (CC: 202–03) draws on the tradition of medieval satires and allegorical poems where birds were used to represent human affairs. The eagle stands for oppression and exploitation of the Gàidhealtachd in many guises, and the poem consists of a number of episodes showing its activities. At one point, the eagle-priest ('an iolair-shagart') preaches complaisance and meekness, referring to the role of the churches in pacifying the people and turning their minds from their earthly grievances to otherworldly matters. When the eagle ministers talk together, Thomson makes them, in an enjoyable humorous touch, the ministers of the Big Nest and the Little Nest (Nead Mòr agus Nead Beag) – the names sound like actual Highland villages while keeping with the avian imagery.

In another part, the chief eagle addresses chickens, representing the Gaels, announcing that he is their new landlord and that on the merit of the schooling he received on the mountain, everything under and over the roost belongs to him. There are also ducks, old Highland landlords, sitting in the parliament on hereditary vote. The final stanza imagines that only when the nest is empty and the imperial eagle loses his grip will the prophesied strength return to the eagle of the wild – the eagle is not a straightforward image, and there are clearly different sorts of eagles. The golden eagle is one of Scotland's national beasts, and Thomson uses it as a positive symbol of courage and national awareness, both at the end of this particular sequence and in later collections.

Another sequence, 'An Crann' (The Plough) (CC: 208–09), is accompanied by a note which explains that the word 'crann' in Gaelic means 'cross, mast, lot, harp-key, Saltire, etc.', and all these meanings are employed in the sequence. It is also a euphemism for the male sexual organ. The poet's English translation is helpful in identifying which meaning he decides to put forward in each case, but it of course does not have the richness of the original. First, 'an crann' is a plough in the country's soil. The plough must go deep and the arms must be strong, if the process is to yield any crops. In the second stanza, it turns into a harp key, and the speaker remembers that his country's harp, before it was smashed, used to resound with many multi-layered tunes, and that the fingers playing it must be loving and strong. Then the country turns into a living, swelling female body, the speaker's lover, and only a birth can make it well again.

In the fourth stanza, in keeping with the agricultural imagery and the physical perception of the land, the speaker states that his country has many wounds which pine trees can never hide. The meaning of these pine trees covering wounds could be the same as that of MacLean's pine trees in 'Hallaig', where they symbolise the new management of Raasay where commercially profitable pine trees replaced the original woods and people were driven out to make room for hunting estates. The vegetation hiding historical wounds is also reminiscent of Thomson's own clearance poem 'Srath Nabhair'.

In the eighth stanza, the poem assumes the tone and rhythm of a traditional satirical song, imagining the Saltire (An Crann) replacing the Union Jack, and the flag, on the basis of the nickname, is personified and suffers bumps and blushes. In the final stanza, the chosen meaning of 'an crann' is the cross and the national cause is imagined as a journey with a cross to Golgotha, and the speaker maintains that no one can give him and his compatriots what their life lacks unless they carry the cross themselves.

Several poems in the collection refer to particular historical events. 'Ceud Bliadhna sa Sgoil' (One Hundred Years in School) (CC: 198–99) first appeared in *Gairm* under the title '1872–1972'. The dates suggest very clearly that the poem is a comment on the Education (Scotland) Act 1872 that effectively banished Gaelic from Scottish schools by not mentioning it as a language in which education could be carried out. Children were discouraged from using Gaelic in schools, in some cases

punished for speaking it, and it was as late as the 1930s that
the use of a punishment device called the 'maide-crochaidh',
i.e. hanging stick (a humiliating symbol hung around a child's
neck for speaking Gaelic), was reported in Lewis.

Ceud bliadhna sa sgoil
is sinn nar Gaidheil fhathast!
Cò shaoileadh gum biodh an fhreumh cho righinn?
Dhòirt iad eallach leabhraichean oirnn,
is cànanan, eachdraidh choimheach,
is saidheans, is chuir iad maidse riutha.
O abair lasair [...]
Is minig a chunna sinn craobh a chaidh a losgadh –
A! 's ann le fun tha mi,
na biodh eagal oirbh, a luchd-stiùiridh an fhoghlaim,
a chomhairlichean na siorrachd, is a' Bheurla cho math agaibh –
a' fàs –
siud sibh, sguabaibh a' chlann a Steòrnabhagh –
nas braise.

A hundred years in school
and we're Gaels still!
Who would have thought the root was so tough?
They poured a load of books on us,
languages, foreign history,
science, and put a match to them.
O what a blaze [...]
We have often seen a bush that was burnt –
I'm just joking,
have no fear, directors of education,
county councillors, with your fluent English –
growing –
that's right, centralise education in Stornoway –
faster.

The poem opens with an ironic expression of wonder – even after a hundred years of schooling which was either openly hostile or not supportive to Gaelic, the Gaels have retained their identity. Here, as in many other poems and articles, we find Thomson's belief that the identity and the language are deeply intertwined.

The last sentence has a more specific implication in the original. In literal translation, 'sguabaibh a' chlann a Steòrnabhagh' means 'sweep the children to Stornoway', referring to frequent closures of small local schools in Lewis (and in the remote parts of the Gàidhealtachd in general) and centralisation of education in the main towns, such as Stornoway. Such arrangements provide less opportunities to keep Gaelic alive in the communities and lead to depopulation, for when schools close, families are more likely to move away and others are less likely to come in. Thomson frequently discussed the importance of local schooling for the preservation of Gaelic in his editorials for *Gairm*.

Another poem referring to a particular set of events is 'Ola' (Oil) (CC: 186–87), one of the most accomplished poems in the collection. In 1969, oil was discovered in the North Sea: the first major discovery was the Montrose field in 1969, followed by the Forties field in 1970 and the Brent field in 1971. Extraction started six years later, in 1975, when Cruden Bay received the first supply of oil extracted from the North Sea. This historical context forms the background of the poem, which starts as a recollection from childhood:

Nuair a bha mi beag
bhiodh bodach a' tighinn a bhùth mo sheanar
gach là laghail, a dh'iarraidh botal ola:
fear dhe na h-òighean glice 's dòcha –

cha deidhinn an urras nach e òigh a bh' ann co-dhiù –
a bha cumail sùgh ris an t-siobhaig;
bodach ait, a ghàire faisg air,
ach beagan de dh'eagal air roimhn an dorch.

When I was a boy
an old man used to come to my grandfather's shop
every lawful day, for a bottle of oil:
one of the wise virgins perhaps –
a virgin in any case, I daresay –
who kept the lamp-wick wet;
a jolly old man, ready to laugh,
but a little afraid of the dark.

In the first part of the poem, Thomson uses his characteristic conversational tone and presents a benevolent, albeit humorous, portrait of the village character. The Biblical reference generates the humour of the poem – the comparison of the slightly eccentric old bachelor from Lewis, who is afraid he might run out of oil and therefore buys it in excessive quantities, to the scriptural wise virgins, who took good care of their lamps, is greatly amusing.

Tha iad ag ràdh an diugh gu bheil an saoghal-bràth de
    dh'ol' againn
anns an dùthaich bheag seo –
bhig seo, bhog seo? –
gu bheil sinn air bhog ann a lèig ola.
Tha mi 'n dòchas gu ruig an t-siobhag oirre.

They say now that we have an eternity of oil
in this little land –
this toty, flabby land? –

that we are afloat on a lake of oil.
I hope the wick can reach it.

In the second part of the poem, the political message is introduced. The speaker talks on behalf of a national community
which suddenly finds itself afloat on a lake of oil. According
to 'them', the country has 'an eternity of oil'. But the attrib-
utes of the country – little, flabby, toty – together with the
reliance on information 'from the outside', imply that
the country may not be strong enough to take advantage
of the rich natural resources. The speaker expresses his hope
that the wick will reach the oil, combining the image of the
overly prudent old man, the Biblical parable, and North Sea
oil. The wick reaching into the oil reservoirs implies that
the oil could be a source of light. In this way, the oil may
symbolise the overall potential of Scotland, and the wick
the needed determination, strength, courage, and national
self-awareness needed to make full use of it. Together with
'Cisteachan-laighe' (CC: 122–23), this is arguably one of
Thomson's most successful political poems, as it manages to
connect commentary on vital contemporary events with a vivid
sketch from childhood, humour, puns, and political appeal.

Creachadh na Clàrsaich/Plundering the Harp, 1982

Creachadh na Clàrsaich/Plundering the Harp is a volume of
Thomson's collected poems, bringing together the previous
four collections and a section of 'Dàin às Ùr' (Latest Poems)
that had not appeared anywhere else and have often been overlooked for this reason. This part contains one of Thomson's
most remarkable achievements and a highlight of his whole
career, the sequence 'Àirc a' Choimhcheangail' (The Ark of the
Covenant) (CC: 268–69). The sequence consists of seventeen
poems and all of them focus on religion and discuss the strong

connection between evangelical Christianity and the life of
Gaelic-speaking Lewis.

In this sequence Thomson at the same time distances himself
from evangelical religion, in accord with his conviction that
it is something foreign and imposed, but he also stresses the
closeness between the Biblical characters and the worshippers
in Lewis and the way the concepts and ideas have entered
people's everyday life and way of thinking. Christianity in
this sequence assumes a distinctly Lewisian form and flavour;
it is at one and the same time foreign and intensely homely.

Most of the poems address someone intimately: they are not
a distanced commentary but a dialogue with various people,
some of whom are named, some of whom are not, while others
capture childhood memories and snapshots from religious life
in Lewis. The speaker presents himself as one of the community, not as an outsider.

In its use of smells, sounds and images, the sequence exhibits
the delicate sensuousness for which Thomson's best poetry is
noted. The overall tone of the sequence is calm and warm,
although at some points Thomson's characteristic measured
criticism and mischief surface. The poems show a deep appreciation of people who follow a creed that the speaker cannot
or does not want to embrace for himself.

The poem 'An Ceistear' (The Catechist) (CC: 270–71) is an
example of how skilfully Thomson can set a convincing scene
with just a few words. The speaker meets another member of
the community who starts to talk to him about religion.

'An dùil,'
ars an duine caomh rium,
'am bi sinn còmhla ri chèile
anns an t-sìorraidheachd?'
Ceist fhuar ann am meadhon an t-samhraidh.

'Do you expect,'
said the kindly man to me,
'we shall be together
in eternity?'
A cold question in midsummer.

For the speaker, the question is a cold one, a sudden existential leap. He does not think about these matters often and
does not feel certain about them, but the man who asks probably thinks about eternity every day. It is an essential part
of his life.

Bha i na b' fhaisg aire-san,
's bha e 'n geall oirr';
bha an t-àit' ud
dha mar dhachaigh nach do dh'fhidir e
bho thùs òige,
tlàth ann an suaineadh na cuimhne,
seasgair ann am brù mac-meanmain,
ach mireanach mar adhar earraich;

It was closer to him
and he longed for it;
that place
was to him like a home he had not known
since early youth,
warm in the folds of memory,
sheltered in the imagination's womb,
but merry like a spring night-sky;

Thomson associates the man's faith and his expectations of
eternal life with warm and homely images, such as the fire and
the hearth. The man does not live in dread of eternal damnation, but expects eternity will be as a lost home, a place of

happiness and safety. Moreover, he does not question the right and ability of other people to reach it and does not try to convert them forcefully to his own persuasion:

> Bha e 'g iarraidh
> gu lorgadh a chàirdean an t-slighe,
> 's gu ruigeadh iad air a socair fhèin;
> cha robh e cur cabhaig orra,
> chan eil dùil no cabhag anns an t-sìorraidheachd.

> *He wanted*
> *his friends to find the way,*
> *and they would arrive in their own good time;*
> *he did not hustle them,*
> *there is neither expectation nor hustling in eternity.*

The last lines speak about tolerance and respect and there is none of the tendency to forcefully impose one's own belief on others which is frequently alleged to happen with religion in Lewis. The poem ends with one of Thomson's great punch-lines which combines gentle humour with depth of thought.

The contrasting tendency to estrange Christianity from Lewis and at the same time stress its deep rootedness in the minds of the people is evident in the poem 'Dòmhnall Rodaidh' (Donald Roddy) (CC: 270–71).

> Nuair a thogadh tu na sailm
> bha sinn air ar giùlan
> air na pongan slaodach sin
> gu ionad eile:

> *When you began the psalm*
> *we were transported*

on these leisurely notes
to another place:

The first lines evoke the power of that unique Gaelic musical phenomenon – the unaccompanied psalm singing where the precentor gives out the line and the congregation repeats it at much greater length. The result is a startling musical form indigenous to Gaelic Scotland.

The precentor is able to transport the congregation to another place where religion is at the same time homely and intimately known and marvellous and utterly foreign:

leitheach slighe eadar Canàan is Garrabost,
le craobhan iongantach a' fàs às a riasg,
gruth is òr-mheasan air a' bhòrd,
ainmean is àiteachan fad-às,
daoine coigreach le plèid is currac orra,
Rut 's Naòmi am bun na lota,
Iòseph a chaidh a dhìth air an *Iolaire.*

half-way between Canaan and Garrabost,
with marvellous trees growing in the peat,
crowdie and oranges on the table,
far-off names and places,
foreign people wearing plaid and mutch,
Ruth and Naomi at the foot of the croft,
Joseph who was lost on the Iolaire.

Thomson expresses this paradox by a series of paired images: the people are taken half-way between Canaan, the Biblical Promised Land, and Garrabost, a township in the Point district of Lewis; marvellous trees, likely from the Middle East, grow out of the peat; there is crowdie (cottage cheese) and oranges, a fruit rarely to be had in Lewis at the time of Thomson's youth, side by side. Biblical characters are imagined as foreign people, but they wear typical Gaelic clothes such as plaid and mutch and they are like neighbours: Ruth and Naomi, the poor women who actually worked the fields in the Bible, stand at the foot of the croft; Joseph, the beloved lost son of Jacob, becomes one of the young men returning home from the First World War who drowned within sight of the shore during the shipwreck of the *Iolaire* on 1 January 1919. The poem also suggests that the lives, the joys and tragedies of the Gaelic-speaking people in Lewis have much in common with those of the people in the Biblical stories.

In the poem 'Iasgairean' (translated by the poet as 'They Themselves Were Fishermen') (CC: 272–73), the speaker forms a connection between the Biblical characters, the apostles who were fishermen too, and the people whom they were trying to convert, who were close to the earth and acquainted with stones, so that they would naturally understand the power of someone who turns stones into bread and was able to move a big stone from his grave – in the poem, this partly explains the attraction of Christianity and the Biblical stories to the Gaels in Lewis who were used to dealing with stony fields and building from stone. 'A' Bheatha Mhaireannach' (Everlasting Life) (CC: 272–73) speaks about the eponymous concept in connection with Gaelic history, and it lists causes that often shortened the life of the Gaels (such as illnesses common in the region, the Clearances, and participation in the army) and paints a vision of everlasting life which is also thoroughly Gaelic – with fish and porridge, good company, and the singing of psalms and hymns.

The sequence 'Àirc a' Choimhcheangail' also includes the poem 'Iomradh air an Fheadhainn a Chaidh Dhachaigh' (An Intimation of Those Who Have Gone Home/Died) (CC: 278–79), a series of masterly executed short portraits of several people who died, 'went home', as the idiom goes, suggesting that the world is but a passing place, and the true home is eternity. The poem is dated 'a' chiad Shàbaid de January, 1979' (First Sabbath of January, 1979), in deference to those to whom the poem refers. It points out effectively how diverse the individual believers are and how differently religion works in their lives.

The last poem, 'Ùrnaigh' (Prayer) (CC: 282–83), satirically expresses the paradox of the speaker's suspected need to believe, and his unwillingness to be caught in the act of praying. The sequence does not mark Thomson's personal conversion, but it shows an interesting combination of his critical approach to religion as a social phenomenon and its role in the history of Lewis, and his appreciation of and respect for the ordinary people who adhere to it, a division which is consistent with opinions Thomson expressed in interviews and essays. It also challenges the image of Evangelical Christianity as something endemic to Lewis and the image of the people as bigoted, unhappy, and intolerant, and presents a more diverse and complex view.

Several poems from the 'Dàin às Ùr' comment on political issues again. The poem 'Alba *v.* Argentina, 2/6/79' (Scotland *v.* Argentina, 2/6/79) (CC: 264–65) is subtitled 'mìos às dèidh Taghadh na Pàrlamaid, 3/5/79' (a month after the General Election, 3/5/79). The poem contrasts the upsurge of patriotic feeling connected with a football match, when the streets of Glasgow were choked with tartan, with the result of the General Election. It ironically depicts the drunken fans as clansmen and their shouting 'Scotland, Scotland' as a battle cry. The final rhymed couplet makes the derisive point 'Alba chadalach, / mìos ro fhadalach' (Sleepy Scotland, / a month late). The speaker clearly sees the patriotic feeling as misplaced: the love of the country is clearly limited to football – a sport of which the poet was otherwise a keen follower – and does not extend as far as voting for a step towards independence.

The short poem 'Rabaidean' (Rabbits) (CC: 260–61) is a return to an older style of a specific image into which a symbolic meaning is added with a light touch at the end – the poem depicts a rabbit crossing the road and almost reaching safety, but when a car arrives and the creature sees the headlights, it becomes afraid and turns back. The speaker then addresses the reader and casually remarks that there is a 'sermon', i.e. a message to be learnt, in Scottish rabbits this year. In the English translation, the date 1979 is added in brackets to make the reference to the referendum on devolution more explicit. Scottish people who did not vote for devolution are compared to rabbits, turning back when headlights dazzle them.

Smeur an Dòchais/Bramble of Hope, 1991

Thomson's sixth book of poetry, *Smeur an Dòchais/Bramble of Hope*, appeared in 1991, nine years after the collected poems and fourteen years after *Saorsa agus an Iolaire*, and it marks a distinct move towards the multicultural world of Glasgow. It is a diverse, very contemporary and very European collection – it captures Glasgow absorbing people from abroad and incorporates Romania, Ukraine, Germany, and France. It is lighter and more hopeful in tone than *Saorsa agus an Iolaire*, and it contains some of the best poems of the later part of Thomson's career.

In *Smeur an Dòchais*, Glasgow is the centre of attention of the first poem, 'Air Stràidean Ghlaschu' (On Glasgow Streets) (SD: 10–11), a sequence consisting of eighteen individual short poems that offer diverse glimpses of the city and its people. There is a long tradition of writing about the city in Gaelic. Especially in traditional songs, the city was seen as a place of exile and contrasted with the lost promised 'land of bens and glens'. Thomson's writing partly belongs to this rich tradition, for he is also an exile, but he accepts his new location and, instead of looking back, he fixes his observant eye on his current home.

As Lewis was sometimes personified as a lover and as a mother, Glasgow is described in distinctly human and feminine terms in the first two items of the sequence. However, there is nothing like the intimate, amorous, sensual attachment to the place in the case of Glasgow: the city is observed and listened to, not touched and smelled as the island was.

> Glaschu
> rocach
> 's am peant a' sgàineadh
> 'na seasamh
> cugallach
> air cnapan àrda.

> *Glasgow*
> *wrinkled*
> *with the paint cracking*
> *standing*
> *unsteadily*
> *on high heels.*

> Sùilean dubha,
> teannaichte,
> an craiceann dlùth air cnàmh na gruaidhe,
> tana, sìolte,
> sùilean beaga piante
> Ghlaschu
> a' coimhead neonitheachd na sìorraidheachd.

> *Dark eyes,*
> *strained,*
> *the skin tight on the cheekbone,*

thin, drained,
the little pained eyes
of Glasgow
observing the nothingness of eternity.

This personification sets the tone for the rest of the sequence, where Glasgow will be presented as unsteady, a little unhealthy and by no means glamorous, but still possessing a certain charm and the will to live. The eyes of Glasgow, 'observing the nothingness of eternity', introduce the existential dimension of the poems, for they are also a search for something that would unite all the fragments into a more meaningful whole, although Thomson seems to be far from believing that such a unifying concept could be easily realised.

The sixteen poems which follow delineate different aspects of the city through miniature portraits of its people. On his walks through the city, the speaker observes, among others, a shoeless man eating an onion (SD: 10–11), beautiful Burmese girls in a café (SD: 14–15) and a drunken vagrant 'preaching' to indifferent people who pass him in their cars (SD: 16–17). The sequence is full of random and disquieting encounters that characterise modern city life.

In poem 6 (SD: 14–15), waitresses in a cafe talk about TV shows, sing a song by John Lennon and seem to be blissfully unaware of their country's dramatic history, which is a source of considerable discomfort to the speaker, who reminiscences on the dead heroes of the past, such as William Wallace and Alasdair Mac Colla, and concludes that his country's present-day pitiful state is caused by ignorance (''s an dùthaich agam, le dìth tuigse, / air a dhol a thaigh na bidse': and my country, for lack of will, / has gone to hell). It is difficult to imagine the waitresses singing 'Alasdair Mhic Cholla Ghasta' and discussing the relative merits of Blind Harry's epic poem while serving the customers, and Thomson is too great a realist to require them to, but the situation serves as a synecdoche of the overall situation of the country when its rich history and culture are being forgotten and replaced by popular culture of disputable quality.

Poem 15 (SD: 22–23) again underlines the multicultural life of Glasgow, this time in the form of Italian culture and cuisine, as the warm Italian talk surrounds the speaker close to the centre of the city, in one of the 'new Italies' in Glasgow. The speaker expresses his conviction that there may be a Caruso in a taverna somewhere and 'ma tha Dante fhathast ann / chan eil fad aige ri dhol / gus a lorg e Inferno' (if a Dante survives / he doesn't have far to go / to find an Inferno). It does not take long to find an Inferno in the city, but it also contains the speaker's Paradise: 'ach tha mo Pharadiso-sa caillte / am badeigin an Glaschu' (but my Paradiso is lost / somewhere in Glasgow).

This move from the otherworldly concerns of Dante's *Commedia* to the Glasgow streets reveals another dimension of the sequence. The city, though portrayed through a collection of commonplace images that are anything but exalted, becomes a venue for existentialist questionings where inferno is easily accessible and where one's personal paradise is hidden, but it seems it has not been lost beyond recovery. In the two following poems (16 and 17), the speaker's private, unspecified pain, as well as his concern for the city, for the nation it represents and for their future, are expressed against the background of the streets. The last poem (18) (SD: 24–25) is profoundly oblique, addressing probably a ghost who walks the streets of Glasgow in search of something. The recovery is difficult because the sought thing is elusive and because there is mist in the streets: 'Chan eil e furasd / a lorg a-rithist / a-measg nan clachan' (It isn't easy / to find it again / among the stones); 'Tha e duilich / làmh a chur ann / anns a' cheò seo' (It is difficult / to put your finger on it / in this mist).

The sequence that started with the thin, dark-eyed Glasgow staring into the nothingness of eternity closes with this enigmatic search for something that is lost in the mist on the city streets, packed and lonely at the same time. Could it be the identity of Glasgow and its people, perhaps of Scotland as a whole, which would turn the fortunes of the city and stop the decay portrayed in the collection? However difficult the search is, the discovery is not deemed impossible, and thus the conclusion is not entirely hopeless. Given Thomson's life-long adherence to Scottish nationalism, this 'something' lost in the streets of Glasgow may be a distinct Scottish national awareness.

The following poem, 'Madainn Diardaoin, ann an Oifis Puist an Glaschu' (Thursday Morning, in a Glasgow Post Office) (SD: 26–27), reads as a postscript to the sequence. It presents another unappealing view of Glasgow: 'na bacaich agus na ciorramaich' (the lame and the halt) gathering at the post office to collect their benefits. The Biblical imagery of the poem elevates Glasgow to something more, to a universal city where the essence of poverty and destitution may be encountered, but this elevation is at the same time undermined by a great deal of irony, such as when the speaker looks to see if Christ is sitting behind the counter or when he compares the unemployment benefits to 'fuaran an fhàsaich' (the spring in the desert).

Some of the poems still go back to Lewis, but it becomes one topic among others, not the obsession of *An Rathad Cian*. One of the most remarkable poems connected to Lewis in *Smeur an Dòchais* is a short poem 'Hòl, air Atharrachadh' (Hòl, Changed) (SD: 98–99), which goes back to the long descriptive poem 'Mu Chrìochan Hòil' (In the Vicinity of Hòl) from *Eadar Samhradh is Foghar*. Twenty-four years later, the same hillock is revisited in this poem, small in terms of scale but far-reaching in terms of implications.

Is gann gu faca mi Hòl am bliadhna,
bha e air fàs cho beag;
feumaidh gu robh 'n Cruthaighear trang
leis an tarbh-chrann,
a' sgrìobadh a' mhullaich dheth
a bha cho àrd 's cho fionnar
's ga chàradh aig a' bhonn,
a' toirt air falbh a chaisead,
agus is dòcha a mhaise,
ga lìomhadh gus a robh a chruth
air a chall.

Air a neo
's ann ormsa bha E 'g obair.

'S mas ann
dè eile rinn E orm?

I hardly noticed Hòl this year,
it has become so small a hill;
the Creator must have been busy
with the bulldozer
scraping away its summit
that was so high and so fresh
and depositing it at the foot,
robbing it of its steepness
and perhaps of its beauty,
smoothing it until its lines
were lost.

Alternatively
He was at work on me.

And if so, what else
did He do to me?

'Hòl, air Atharrachadh' may be read as Thomson's innovative take, at the same time humorous and moving, on the traditional Gaelic theme of 'caochladh' (adverse change) both in people and in nature where a location is revisited and its change for the worse is observed. The speaker revisits a place he used to be intimately acquainted with and he gives an account of the alterations he perceives in the place: its diminished distinctiveness, its loss of beauty. Since the notion of the Creator working on the hillock with a bulldozer, however novel and radical, is implied as unrealistic, the speaker's attention turns to himself. The change in his perception of the place leads to the reflection on how much he has changed throughout the years. The place once again serves as a reflective screen for individual psychological developments, as a sieve in which the passing of time may be, at least for a moment, captured and inspected.

Although it deals with some weighty topics, *Smeur an Dòchais*, as the title indicates, is indeed a collection with a restrained hopeful air about it. Not that it is excessively optimistic, but in comparison with the obsessive concerns of *An Rathad Cian* and the gloom and bitterness of *Saorsa agus an Iolaire*, it is much more relaxed. There are no signs, however, of Thomson getting lax in his comments on the politics and culture of Scotland.

Meall Garbh/The Rugged Mountain, 1995

In its broad mixture of topics, *Meall Garbh/The Rugged Mountain* resembles *Smeur an Dòchais*, but while the 1991 collection had a distinct Glaswegian focus, the title of the 1995 collection announces a return to Perthshire, a region which Thomson often visited on family holidays during childhood and adolescence and where he also lived for some time. A number of poems discuss, in various combinations, the topics of Scottish and Gaelic identity in the contemporary world, the loss of historical and cultural awareness, the corrupting influence of tabloid media and consumerism, and the inscrutable ups and downs of history. While *Smeur an Dòchais* was remarkably fresh and spirited, the sixth collection does not entirely live up to the standard of its immediate predecessor.

One of the most remarkable poems in the collection, however, is 'Feòrag Ghlas, Tuath air Braco' (Grey Squirrel, North of Braco) (MG: 14–15), in which Thomson handles the theme of the complex cultural history of Scotland with humour and points out that Gaelic culture, which has been in many places overcome and supressed, had itself ousted other cultures in the past. Braco is a village in Perthshire and the speaker recalls driving through the landscape and encountering a grey squirrel – a species originally from North America which is considered invasive in Europe, as it aggressively replaces the native red and brown squirrels.

A' siubhal tron an dùthaich bhrèagh sin
chunna mi feòrag a' teicheadh bhon a rathad:
tè ghlas a bh' ann, an treubh ùr tha sgaoileadh
tro dhùthaich nan Cruithneach,
gun eòlas aic' air na lùban dìomhair
no air an t-saighead a tha roinn na cloiche,
beò air a crìochan fhèin,
beò air cnothan a' gheamhraidh,
is freumhaichean, corra ugh is iseanan beaga,
is uaireannan a' milleadh chraobhan
leis an dèidh aic' air an rùsg.
'S ann à Ameireagaidh a thàinig a sinnsreachd,
's thuirt i rium, tha mi 'n dùil,
ged nach duirt mise guth,
'Carson nach tiginn a seo;

chaidh gu leòr dhe na daoin' agaibhse
a-null thugainne.'

Travelling through that bonny countryside
I saw a squirrel running away from the road:
a grey one, the new tribe colonising
the land of the Picts,
unaware of the mysterious loops
or the arrow dividing the stone-face,
living in its own territory,
surviving on winter nuts,
and roots, an occasional egg and small chicks,
and sometimes destroying trees
through its fondness of the bark.
Her ancestors came from America,
and I think she said to me –
though I hadn't spoken,
'Why shouldn't I come here;
plenty of your people
went to our country.'

The impertinent squirrel who reminds the speaker of the extensive Scottish emigration to North America adds a humorous touch to the poem and also provides a means to further the central argument.

Tha a shearmon fhèin aig gach neach
's cha duirt mise rithe ach 'Glè cheart,'
ach air a shon sin
bha mi a' smaoineachadh air na Cruithnich
a dh'fhàg am breacadh de 'pheitean'
air an dùthaich seo
('s ann an trì mionaidean

chaidh mi seachad air tuathanas
air a bheil an t-ainm *Pett* fhathast);
is beag a bha dhùil ac'
gun teicheadh an fheòrag ruadh
roimhn a' pheasan ghlas seo,
no gun cuireadh Gaidheil às dhan
a' chainnt acasan, 's gu fàsadh na Gaidheil fhèin
rudeigin Sagsanach.

Everyone has his own sermon
and all I said was 'Quite right,'
but for all that
I kept thinking of the Picts
who dotted this countryside with 'petts'
(and in three minutes
I passed a farm
which is still called 'The Pett');
they had no idea
that the red squirrel would retreat
at the coming of this grey pest,
nor that the Gaels would eradicate
their language,
and that the Gaels themselves would become
somewhat like the Saxons.

The speaker agrees the squirrel's argument is right, but he keeps thinking about the fact that the Gaels overcame the Picts and obliterated their language and their culture, which only remain present in the carved stones and place names. The poem thus shows a full awareness that the Gaelic situation is not unique – the Gaels also emigrated abroad and took other people's land, and therefore should not be, as the squirrel points out, too offended when people from abroad come and settle in their lands.

In the end the speaker points out that the Picts would have been quite surprised to see the Gaels themselves succumbing to another influence – that of the English. The poem evinces chilling acknowledgement that the Gaels, their culture and language, however dear they are to the speaker's own heart, are just one example among many, subject to the same laws of change. This is one of Thomson's finest poems dealing with topics of cultural dominance, both in terms of the level-headedness and humour of its approach.

Sùil air Fàire/Surveying the Horizon, 2007

In the last collection published during Thomson's lifetime, *Sùil air Fàire/Surveying the Horizon*, all concerns and influences that have been present in the seventy years of the poet's career are represented. It is not only an old man's eye surveying the horizon of future things it will not live to see, but also the eye of the poet looking back over his life's work. The exploration is prospective as much as retrospective, and, in some aspects, the collection also features new perspectives on old topics and fresh approaches.

One might expect Thomson's final collection to be some sort of testament and a sample book of his verse with little innovation. Some of the poems do indeed follow patterns and themes introduced in *Smeur an Dòchais* and *Meall Garbh* and may seem repetitive. Some of the old themes, however, become more prominent than ever before in *Sùil air Fàire*, such as meditations on the inscrutability of history, the ever-changing nature of the world, the impact of consumer culture and the media on Scotland, and the multicultural realities of the late twentieth and early twenty-first century. The focus on the changing world, concerned and cautious but not negative and even slightly curious, is also evident in Thomson's editorials for the last issues of *Gairm,* which were probably written at the same time as some of the poems.

Another of the old themes becomes very prominent in this volume: Gaelic, its precarious position and the inevitable make-believe associated with some efforts to revive the language. Such focus is understandable given the retrospective function of the collection and the poet's awareness of the fact that he is not going to witness the future fortunes of the language and will soon be unable to contribute to its development.

In 'Àros nan Sean?' (Old Folks' Home?) (SF: 18–19), Thomson presents a particularly bitter, dismal image of the gradual withering of the Gaelic language and of the efforts to strengthen it: in a care home built with money from the National Lottery, the old and infirm will be supported by apparatus so that they can mumble 'Suas leis a' Ghàidhlig!' (Up with the Gaelic!) to the accompaniment of harp music. The origin of this dreary vision is outlined in connection with place names as the speaker is surprised that the gradual decline of Gaelic he had witnessed elsewhere has reached places in Lewis as well:

tachdadh sa bhràighe
is ciorram an ceòs
liota san teanga [...]
is monbar am mùirneig
's na cnàmhan gu bhith ris
a-nis.

choking at the Bràighe/throat
and maiming in Keose/the hollow
lisping in Tong/the tongue [...]
and mumbling at Mùirneag/the loved one,
and the bones just about showing
in Ness/now.

This elaborate word play, where the place names oscillate between their function as place names and their meanings as ordinary nouns, although explained in the translation, is designed to be appreciated by a fluent/native speaker of the language to whom these words will delineate both the actual localities and the meanings behind the names. A person acquainted with Lewis, moreover, will be able to associate the images of withering and decay of the language with the specific communities. This poem about language thus becomes a test of what it imagines: when the word play cannot be appreciated, the loss has actually come.

In 'Nuair a Dh'fhalbhas a' Ghàidhlig' (When Gaelic Goes) (SF: 50–51), Thomson imagines Scotland without Gaelic – the language will become another dinosaur, something to be excavated centuries later and written about frantically in the media, and scientists will research its impact on the country, and with the latest technology they will perhaps hear a couple of songs, striving with prayers and poetry, rising from this old land. Issues concerning Gaelic feature in many other poems in the collection, such as in 'Soidhne nan Tìm' (The Sign of the Times*) (SF: 22), 'Cridhe an t-Sluaigh' (The Heart of the People*) (SF: 23), 'Teagamh' (Doubt*) (SF: 30) and elsewhere. In these poems, Thomson voices his suspicions of some efforts to promote the language, although he often advocated them in his journalism: putting Gaelic on TV and on road signs, when it is actually dying in the communities and when it loses contact with its natural environment, emerges as specious ('Dh'fhalbh Siud is Thàinig Seo') (That Went and This Came*) (SF: 48). For Thomson, this is not a question of being threatened by non-native speakers of Gaelic or of the language being moved to new areas of life – the evidence of his support for these innovations is plentiful in his articles and *Gairm* editorials – but rather, as often, a question of standard and quality.

Many of his poems about Gaelic revolve around the question of authenticity – how far can one go with the revivalist efforts until they rob a language of its authenticity? When does a language stop being authentic? Introducing bilingual road signs is a fine idea, as it reminds people about the existence of Gaelic, and about the origin of many Scottish place names. But, Thomson seems to ask, does this policy not become a mere cover-up for reluctance to use the language in everyday life? What difference does it make to have Gaelic on TV when it is not fluent, correct Gaelic, and when the intended audiences of such programmes keep on talking to one another in English?

A more comforting view, similar in tone to that of 'Nuair a Thig a' Bhalbhachd' (When Stillness Comes) (MG: 84–85) and 'Ceòl' (Music) (SD: 96–97), emerges from the poem 'A' Siubhal nam Blàth' (Reconnoitering the Blossoms) (SF: 94–95) when he imagines Gaelic only 'half-dead' on the pages of books and thinks it possible that it will blossom in people's hearts as a language of learning and literature, if not of everyday communication. The section 'Leòdhas A-rithist' (Lewis Again) also features reflections on the future of the Western Isles and the Gaelic culture: 'Riasg?' (Peat-Moss?) (SF: 14–15); 'Usgairean' (Jewels) (SF: 24–25); 'Seann Daoimean' (An Ancient Diamond) (SF: 36–37). The future and the preservation of what is valuable in the past seem to be more important than looking back.

The special role of Glasgow in Thomson's writing and life, which has been posited earlier, is confirmed in the second section of *Sùil air Fàire*. The poems it contains again comment on the multi-faceted nature of the city, as the very title of the first poem, 'Glaschuan (Glasgows) (SF: 64–65), suggests. It is the city of the rich and the poor, the powerful and the downtrodden, a crossroads of different nationalities and languages. Thomson does not content himself with general observations and sometimes zooms in very close to see the specific features of the city, such as 'eaglaisean a' caochladh gu taighean-seinnse' (churches changing to pubs) and 'ball-coise a' strì ri creideamh' (football at odds with religion).

For example, the poem 'Glaschu nan Cinneach' (Glasgow of the Foreigners) (SF: 90–91) is another glance at the multi-cultural vortex of Glasgow: the Italians, the Chinese, Indian dresses, Jewish hats, a Gael from Uist and a nun. The speaker proceeds to ask how long it will take until a Turkish mother in Glasgow calls her daughter by the traditional Lowland name 'Senga', and points out the historical 'successes' of an unde-fined group of the people (the Gaels? the Scots? the people of Glasgow?), including the defeat of the Picts, the Welsh and 'corra Shasannach' (occasional English folk), and concludes with a tongue-in-cheek observation – 'ged nach d' fhuair sinn smachd air na h-Èireannaich fhathast' (though we still haven't controlled the Irish). This is both a comment on the inability of the people to resist invasion and on their succumbing too easily to foreign influences, and a general observation on the speed of assimilation in big cities. Another interesting poem from this section is 'Uaigneas a' Bhaile-mhòir' (City Loneliness) (SF: 80–81), which lends an ear to the different voices of the city: the Glasgow vernacular as echoed in James Kelman's novels and the voice of an old Gael from Harris remembering his home are heard among a multitude of others. The closing remark on the 'lusan ùra / a' tighinn beò às an fhàsach' (new plants / appear from the wilderness) and the possibility of change coming every morning suggests the open future of the city.

There are many links between the Glasgow poems of *Sùil air Fàire* and *Smeur an Dòchais*. However, contrasting the Gaels and the other incomers to Glasgow is absent here, and it also seems that the poet's perspective broadens from the Gaels to Scots in general. Although he does not stop being worried about the city and the nation, the poet's view of the city and its future seems to be slightly more hopeful, as if the mist that complicated the search at the end of 'Air Stràidean Ghlaschu' (SD: 24–25) has lifted.

The section 'Laoich' (Champions) celebrates some of Thomson's heroes. The inclusion of 'Alasdair Mac Mhaighstir Alasdair' (SF: 140–41) is not surprising, but the usual pantheon is broadened to include some of Thomson's contemporaries. One of them is the great poet 'Ùisdean MacDhiarmaid' (Hugh MacDiarmid) (SF: 142–43), whom he addresses especially in relation to his revival of Scots and praises him for lifting 'fallaing na meirge / bho ulaidhean àrsaidh' (lifting the mantle of rust / from age-old treasures). Although MacDiarmid forsook his Scots projects and wrote in English in the later stages of his career, it was thanks to him that new skin would form under the cracks on the bruised spirit of Scottish heritage, and his achievement will live on and even the blind will see its beauty. The poem is thoroughly positive and conciliatory – the controversial aspects of MacDiarmid's life and career are overlooked in favour of what was good and lasting in them, of what should survive. It also reflects Thomson's increased interest in Scots in the latest phase of his career and the importance he assigned to its revival and development, alongside Gaelic, to the future of Scotland. In the poem 'A' Chuimhne' (Memory*) (SF: 162), he adds Lowland people to the pantheon: William Dunbar side by side with Mac Mhaighstir Alasdair, followed by MacDiarmid, the philosopher David Hume and the painter Henry Raeburn.

Sùil air Fàire reads like a sample book of Thomson's oeuvre: it is diverse, wide-ranging and attests to the proverbial Gaelic statement made by the speaker in 'Sràid Bhochanain, Glaschu' – ''S iomadh rud a chì am fear a bhios fada beò' (Much can be seen by him whose life is long) (SF: 74–75). It is an overview of the past, but it also proves that even here Thomson is developing as a poet: he follows the directions outlined in previous books and goes further, giving prominence to themes that have been present but have never been brought forward to such an extent.

As a whole, *Sùil air Fàire* gives the impression of being remarkably relaxed and self-possessed. There is quiet melancholy and genuine fondness in the farewell to beloved places and people, but also humour; not only acknowledgment of past losses and present troubles, but also resilient hope and a keen surveying of future horizons.

5. *GAIRM* AND PROSE WRITINGS

Thomson had a lifelong interest in journalism. His magazine debut was entitled the *Bayble Herald*, which he, 'admittedly for very local circulation' (meaning his parents, brother, and family friends), edited and issued in the Bayble schoolhouse for several years from about the age of ten.[10] Large sketches of Cotrìona Mhòr, a local lady who came to help with the cleaning and is the subject of Thomson's fine poem in *An Rathad Cian* (CC: 158–59), filled the space when 'copy was short and inspiration failed'. His second venture into journalism was the student nationalist magazine *Alba Mater*, which he co-founded in 1945 at Aberdeen. Six years later he embarked on a journalistic project which proved to be one of the crowning achievements of his career, a venture of profound influence on the Gaelic world, and also a forum where his political opinions and his vision of the Gaelic revival could be both discussed and carried out in poetry, essays and other forms – the quarterly *Gairm* (1952–2002). The magazine is considered the basis of the revival of Gaelic literature in the second half of the twentieth century and the first part of the new infrastructure which helped to develop modern poetry and the short story in Gaelic.

The project started in 1951 when Thomson approached Finlay J. Macdonald (Fionnlagh Dòmhnallach, 1925–1987) of the Gaelic department of the BBC with the idea of establishing a Gaelic quarterly magazine. Since the two editors managed to secure funds from individual people, the magazine

---

10 Derick Thomson, 'A Man Reared in Lewis', 135; Derick Thomson, 'Some Recollections', 57. Thomson talks about his childhood journalistic ventures in the documentary film *Creachadh na Clàrsaich* that also shows some pages from his hand-written and hand-drawn periodicals. See the bibliography for full references.

was independent and it allowed them to express radical views on many issues. The first issue of *Gairm* appeared in autumn 1952, the last one in autumn 2002, which means that the quarterly was an important force in the Gaelic world for fifty years. Thomson was clearly the major instigator of the whole venture. Various other revivalist activities were associated with *Gairm*, such as setting up Gaelic classes for children in Glasgow and establishing a publishing house, Gairm Publications, which produced poetry, fiction and various textbooks and dictionaries.

The title 'Gairm' means 'call, calling, call of the cockerel', and the cockerel was the symbol of the magazine and appeared on the cover. (Later on, a cartoon of two cockerels with a typewriter was used as a heading for the editorial.) The voice of the cockerel was loudly calling for a Gaelic revival and strengthening of the language in all areas of life.

Thomson and Macdonald were ready to make compromises so that the magazine would attract a substantial readership, and therefore diluted the sometimes radical new writing with more light-hearted or traditional pieces. *Gairm* thus contained travel writing, crosswords, advertisements and pages dedicated to fashion and cosmetics, songs, portrayals of important people in the Gaelic world with photos, humorous stories and traditional poetry.

When recalling the beginnings of the magazine, Thomson mentioned that they wanted to open it to various writing styles, to have both traditional writing and new literature. This literary side of the magazine became more prevalent in the last decades. Some of the most important pieces of modern writing in Gaelic appeared in *Gairm* for the first time, for example Sorley MacLean's 'Hallaig' in 1954, and the first Gaelic poems of Iain Crichton Smith and Christopher Whyte. In its early years, *Gairm* organised a short story competition (*Gairm* 34, winter 1960) and it was certainly one of the main outlets thanks to which the short story gained such prominence in Gaelic literature in the second half of the twentieth century.

Gairm also proved to be an important medium for translations from other languages into Gaelic, for example translations of short stories from Irish (Pádraig Ó Conaire) and French (Guy de Maupassant), Christopher Whyte's translations of European poetry (Anna Akhmatova, Konstantinos Kavafis, Janis Ritsos) and also rather surprising pieces, such as an extract from Tolkien's *The Silmarillion*. It published articles on current topics of all sorts, reviews of new books, essays on history, folklore, literature, and indeed any other topic, as part of the general effort to prove that Gaelic was flexible enough to accommodate ideas reflecting the modern world and to support the Gaels to take more interest in their own region, in Scotland, and the world.

In his essay 'The Role of the Writer in a Minority Culture', Thomson pointed out that 'a minority culture, with its tendency to ingrowing, and its incipient persecution complex, should be subjected to satire periodically. A society that can learn to laugh at itself becomes more resilient, and the minority cultures need all the resilience they can muster.'[11] The editorials in *Gairm* were certainly doing their best to provide such satirical impulses and boost social resilience. Another point raised by Thomson in the essay is that 'the minority writer should cultivate a tougher skin, and should not be afraid of speaking his mind, even if by so doing he drives himself into some sort of voluntary exile'. This too was to an extent true for the editors of *Gairm*, for they certainly did not hesitate to speak their mind and openly criticised various bodies and the Gaels as a people, for example for being too stingy or lazy to buy Gaelic books, or for being too shy or cowardly to stand up to defend their rights and their heritage.

11 Derick Thomson, 'The Role of the Writer in a Minority Culture', *Transactions of the Gaelic Society of Inverness* XLIV (1964–1966), p. 270.

Gairm decidedly strove to use Gaelic for contemporary and new topics, publishing articles about the Vietnam War, the situation of the Kurds in Iran, and essays on the philosophy of the Danish thinker Søren Kierkegaard or the works of the Argentinian writer Jorge Luis Borges. As a result of these efforts, the magazine was sometimes criticised for not using sufficiently pure Gaelic and for not being mindful enough of the Gaelic traditions. The editors defended themselves by arguing that their aim was to use contemporary Gaelic, not Gaelic as it was two hundred years before, for it had to be as free as any other language under the sun, free to borrow words if it needed them, and they complained that too many people were trying to make an old woman of Gaelic – trapped in the corsets which she wore in her youth (*Gairm* 7). They also argued that changes in language and literature were not a symptom of crisis and death but rather a sign of life – they could not be conserved as they used to be and it would be damaging to force contemporary poets to write in the same vein all the time.

Thomson, apart from editing the magazine, shaping its editorial policy and inviting contributors, also wrote for the magazine in a number of genres: his poems often appeared first in *Gairm* and only later in collections; five of his short stories were published in the magazine; he provided many of the reviews which appeared in the section 'An Sgeilp Leabhraichean' (The Bookshelf); and he wrote several articles about his travels abroad, produced photo series, and contributed essays on Gaelic literature. His politics found expression in the editorials for the magazine which he was basically using as a vehicle for his own views.

6. CONCLUSION

Derick Thomson shaped Gaelic Scotland more than any other person in the second half of the twentieth century. In many ways, the current activities aimed at strengthening the position of Gaelic in Scotland still follow the patterns outlined by Thomson in his editorials for *Gairm*, in articles and pamphlets, and some of his ideas were so advanced and progressive that what they outlined has not been achieved yet. The same applies to his academic work – his two major achievements, *An Introduction to Gaelic Poetry* and *The Companion to Gaelic Scotland*, remain unsurpassed, and a number of projects he called for have not yet been embarked on. Should one wonder what to do in order to contribute to a better future for Gaelic in Scotland, Derick Thomson's work provides ample inspiration and most of his suggestions and opinions are still relevant to this day.

As a poet, Thomson has produced a large body of work of outstandingly high and consistent quality. He was the first poet to use free verse consistently in Gaelic. His poems, both in terms of form and content, had a profound influence on the following generation of Gaelic poets. His writing about Lewis stands out as the most complex and varied modern contribution to the traditional genre of Gaelic place poetry.

In spite of the amazing scope of his achievements as a poet, scholar, and activist, and his unparalleled contribution to the preservation of Gaelic in Scotland, Thomson seems to have been somewhat neglected both by researchers and the public.

This short book seeks to inspire more engagement with Derick Thomson, believing that his skill and sensitivity as a poet, his fierce commitment and great sense of humour as a journalist, his remarkable intellect and rigour as an academic, his devotion to Gaelic and Scotland and his broad cosmopolitan outlook as an activist still have much to offer to the Gaelic-speaking areas, to Scotland, and to Europe.

7. SELECT BIBLIOGRAPHY

Derick Thomson – Poetry Collections

An Dealbh Briste (Edinburgh: Serif Books, 1951).

Eadar Samhradh is Foghar (Glasgow: Gairm, 1967).

An Rathad Cian (Glasgow: Gairm, 1970).

Saorsa agus an Iolaire (Glasgow: Gairm, 1977).

Creachadh na Clàrsaich/Plundering the Harp (Edinburgh: Macdonald, 1982).

Smeur an Dòchais/Bramble of Hope (Edinburgh: Canongate, 1991).

Meall Garbh/The Rugged Mountain (Glasgow: Gairm, 1995).

Sùil air Fàire/Surveying the Horizon (Stornoway: Acair, 2007).

Derick Thomson – Short Stories

Apart from their original appearance in *Gairm*, some of Thomson's short stories have been reprinted in the following collections:

MacÌomhair, Dòmhnall Iain (ed.). *Eadar Peann is Pàipear* (Glasgow: Gairm, 1984).

MacLeòid, Dòmhnall Iain (ed.). *Dorcha tro Ghlainne* (Glasgow: Gairm, 1970).

Derick Thomson – Interviews, Autobiographical Essays, Recordings, Films

'A Man Reared in Lewis.' *As I Remember: Ten Scottish Authors Recall How Writing Began for Them.* Edited by Maurice Lindsay. London: Robert Hale, 1979. 123–40.

'Some recollections.' *Spirits of the Age: Scottish Self Portraits.* Edited by Paul Henderson Scott. Edinburgh: The Saltire Society, 2005. 55–67.

Derick Thomson, Iain Crichton Smith and Andrew Mitchell. *Taking You Home*: *Poems and Conversations.* Argyll: Argyll Publishing, 2006.

Whyte, Christopher. 'Interviews with Ruaraidh MacThòmais.' *Glasgow: Baile Mòr nan Gàidheal/City of the Gaels.* Edited by Sheila M. Kidd. Glasgow: Roinn na Ceiltis, Oilthigh Ghlaschu, 2007. 239–94.

Bàrdachd le Ruaraidh MacThòmais (cassette and audio CD).
Glasgow: Scotsoun, 2002. With an introduction by John
MacInnes.

Creachadh na Clàrsaich (film documentary). Produced by
Anna Mhoireasdan. Interviews by Fionnlagh MacLeòid.
Eòlas, 2000.

Six Lewis Poems (a video of Derick Thomson reading six of his
poems with translations). Glasgow University Audio-Visual
Services. Directed by Calum Ferguson, c. 1990.

Essays on Derick Thomson and His Works

Black, Ronald. '*Gairm*: An Aois Òir.' *Aiste* 2 (2008). 94–119.
—'Sorley MacLean, Derick Thomson, and the Women Most
Dangerous to Men.' *The Bottle Imp* 21 (July 2017). 1–7.
Byrne, Michel. 'Monsters and Goddesses: Culture Re-energised
in the Poetry of Ruaraidh MacThòmais and Aonghas
MacNeacail.' *The Edinburgh History of Scottish
Literature, Vol. 3. Modern Transformations: New
Identities*. Edited by Ian Brown. Edinburgh: Edinburgh
University Press, 2007. 176–84.
Grimble, Ian. 'The Poet and Scholar as Journalist.' *Scottish
Gaelic Studies* XVII (1996). 159–71.
MacDonald, Ian. 'The Poetry of Derick Thomson.' *Alba
Litteraria: A History of Scottish Literature*.
Ed. Marco Fazzini. Venezie Maestre: Amos Edizioni, 2005.
641–60.
—'Derick Thomson: Poet and Scholar'. *Scottish Language* 37
(2019). 73–90.
MacLeod, Michelle, and Moray Watson. 'Ruaraidh
MacThòmais: the Glasgow Verse.' *Glasgow: Baile Mòr nan
Gàidheal/City of the Gaels*. Ed. Sheila M. Kidd. Glasgow:
Roinn na Ceiltis, Oilthigh Ghlaschu, 2007. 216–27.
Poncarová, Petra Johana. 'Derick Thomson's *An Rathad Cian*
(*The Far Road*, 1970): Modern Gaelic Poetry of Place
between Introspection and Politics'. *The Poetics of Space
and Place in Scottish Literature*. Edited by M. Szuba and J.
Wolfreys. London: Palgrave Macmillan, 2019. 209–29.
—'Nuair a Dh'fhalbhas a' Ghàidhlig (When Gaelic
Goes): Gaelic in the Poetry of Derick Thomson.' *Scottish*

Culture: Dialogue and Self-Expression. Edited by Aniela Korzeniowska and Izabela Szymańska. Warsaw: Semper, 2016. 265–76.

Smith, Iain Crichton. 'The Poetry of Derick Thomson.' *Towards the Human*. Edinburgh: Macdonald Publishers, 1986. 140–43.

Whyte, Christopher. 'Derick Thomson: Reluctant Symbolist.' *Chapman* 38 (1984): 1–6.

—'Derick Thomson: the Recent Poetry.' *Aiste* 1 (2007). 22–37.

—'The Gaelic Renaissance: Sorley MacLean and Derick Thomson.' *British Poetry from the 1950s to the 1990s*. Edited by Gary Day and Brian Docherty. London: Macmillan, 1997. 143–69.

—'The 1970s' in *Modern Scottish Poetry*. Edinburgh: Edinburgh University Press, 2004.

Various contributors. *Mar Chomharra – Ruaraidh MacThòmais aig 90 / Derick Thomson at 90: A Celebration*. Glasgow and Edinburgh: The Gaelic Books Council and The Scottish Poetry Library, 2011.

Electronic Sources on Derick Thomson

Hayes, David. 'Derick Thomson at 90: Gaelic poet in the world.' *Open Democracy*. 5 August 2011. **www.opendemocracy.net/en/derick-thomson-at-90-gaelic-poet-in-world/** (accessed 13 June 2020).

Meek, Donald E. 'Appreciation of Professor Derick S. Thomson: Funeral Oration, as Delivered.' *Passages from Tiree* (personal blog). 5 April 2013. **meekwrite.blogspot.com/2013/04/appreciation-of-professor-derick-s.html** (accessed 13 June 2020).

Ruaraidh MacThòmais / Derick S. Thomson: **ruaraidhmacthomais.wordpress.com** – a website containing information about Derick Thomson's life and work.

An Sgeulachd Ghoirid: **www.ansgeulachdghoirid.com** – a project that makes Gaelic short stories available online with full text, readings, and commentary.

Làrach nam Bàrd: **www.bbc.co.uk/alba/foghlam/larachnam-bard** – Gaelic website dealing with the most important poets, including interviews, reviews, and poems.

Scottish Poetry Library: **www.scottishpoetrylibrary.org.uk/ poetry/poets/derick-thomson** – short introductory article about Thomson, poems in Gaelic and English.

Tobar an Dualchais/Kist o Riches: **www.tobarandualchais.co.uk** – online archive of Scottish tradition, includes several recordings of Thomson reading his own poems, talking about various issues, and singing traditional Gaelic songs.